The *New York Times* said: "THE SECRET LIFE OF JESUS has a charm and freshness . . . which will engage the reader's interest and deserves the time it takes to read it."

AN INCREDIBLE RECORD
OF SUPPRESSED HISTORY

A man of sorrows, despised and rejected, Jesus lived and died to bring light and freedom to the world.

For centuries the true story has been distorted and repressed.

Finally the fearless Upton Sinclair, who has for over sixty years fought the battle of truth for all men, has written a full account of *The Secret Life of Jesus.*

We are proud to bring to you this chance of acquainting yourself with the real meaning and purpose of the greatest life ever lived by a single person on this earth.

It is a tale of burning love, rarest heroism, magnificent adventure and deepest tragedy. Upton Sinclair alone, with his versatility and perception, could have done this justice to the theme. As you read it, you will be amazed at how little you really know about Jesus who said, "I am the Light and the Way."

Upton Sinclair

The Secret Life
Of Jesus

The Secret Life
Of Jesus

Upton Sinclair

Reprinted By
Synergy International of The Americas
333 W. 17th St., Suite 3
Dubuque, Iowa 52001

ISBN: 1934-5681-8-X

THE SECRET
LIFE OF JESUS

CONTENTS

PREFACE

THERE are learned men who deny that Jesus called the Christ is an historic figure; that such a man ever lived and died on earth. I have considered their arguments, but cannot accept them, and for a special reason: that, as a student and creator of fiction, I recognize, or believe that I recognize in the Gospel narratives the presence of a personality. I meet there a man of loving-kindness, and at the same time of energy and passion; a man hating injustice and fighting for righteousness. Such a personality cannot have come into existence by accident, or by the accumulation of any number of Orphic and Mithraic and Egyptian sun-god myths.

It is this man I have attempted to portray; and the portrayal automatically divides itself into three parts. First: his life up to the age of twenty-five or thirty. Concerning this we are told very little, and the task therefore becomes one of creative imagination. I have asked myself, as a novelist, what would have been the childhood and youth of such a man? What would have been his environment? What teachers would have shaped his mind and prepared him to become a world figure? I have set down my guesses, and you, the reader, will be the judge of my success or failure.

Second: his period of a year or two as teacher and man of action. Concerning this we have four written records, frequently contradictory and of highly dubious text. I have studied these with one aim in mind, to discover the real man in them. I have chosen those episodes which seem to me to bear the stamp of inner truth. I have tried not to trouble the reader with controversy, but to tell a straightforward story, letting the great soul speak for himself.

Third: His life after he gave up the ghost on the cross. He has continued to live in the memory of men, and through nineteen centuries his spirit has moved them. As with all ancient characters, the myth-makers set to work upon him at once; the forgers labored piously upon his record; the sectarians tore at him, the superstitious and the seekers of power used him for their purposes. For nineteen hundred

9

years this struggle has gone on; it has been a world struggle, having the destinies of mankind tied up with it.

This part of the story of Jesus cannot be told without controversy, for controversy is the very essence of it. What I have done is to study the arguments and tell the truth as I see it; and again you, the reader, must be the judge. Do the best you can, for whoever you are, and wherever you live, what you believe about Jesus, called the Christ, is a matter of moment to you. I am not talking about your immortal soul, but about your welfare and happiness here on earth. Jesus surely lives; and the place where he lives is in your heart and mine.

Let me add a few words as to my qualifications for the task. I was brought up as a devout Protestant Episcopal boy. At the age of thirteen or fourteen I was teaching a Sunday-school class in the Church of the Holy Communion in New York. I attended services every day of the forty days of Lent, and this, not because I was told to, but of my own impulse. I read the Bible through several times, and when I began to study foreign languages, I made it a part of my task to read the New Testament in each language, Latin, Greek, German, French, and Italian.

I left the church at the age of sixteen, but I have never left Jesus. I have written about him frequently, especially in *The Profits of Religion,* and in the novel, *They Call Me Carpenter,* in which I brought him to the city of Los Angeles as I knew it after the first World War, the time of the I.W.W., the American Legion, and the 'Red Squad.' A little later I did the same thing with his mother in a novelette called *Our Lady,* which, although it is loving and reverent, displeased the orthodox. Having written forty novels and a dozen plays, I have had practice in the delineation of character, and this constitutes a special kind of training for the study of controverted texts. I have ventured to say, "This is what Jesus would have said"; and again, "This is an interpolation; he never would have said it."

I hold him for one of the greatest of men, and have written about him with love and an open mind. Unless you, the reader, are a learned scholar, you will find statements that are new to you and seem strange. My advice is, take them as part of a story and read on. Toward the end you will find my reasons for believing that they represent the truth, or at any rate the best guess which can be made with our present knowledge.

I add this interesting detail. A Gallup poll published March 31, 1950, disclosed that fifty-three per cent of Americans were unable to name the author of any *one* of the four Gospels. A second question was asked, and it was found that only thirty-six per cent could name the authors of all four. From this it appears that many of my readers will be making the acquaintance of Jesus for the first time. That would seem to be reason enough for the book's existence.

BOOK ONE

YOUTH

❀   ❀   ❀

1

IN THE dry hot lands which lie to the east of the Sea of Galilee and the River Jordan there wandered throughout Old Testament times various tribes of people, some called Rechabites and some Kenites, or Cainites; they wore upon their foreheads a black cross which was the mark of Cain— but it was no disgrace, on the contrary it was a caste mark, a sign that they were of the House of David. They called themselves sons of David, and it is possible that they were right; there were some forty generations between that glorious king and the beginning of the Christian era, and considering the ways of his son Solomon there must have been enough of his descendants to have populated a large portion of Palestine. Through many centuries these people had mingled with the Hebrews, adopted the Hebrew God, and considered themselves of the Hebrew race.

They were migratory workers, known as *harashim,* which is translated carpenters, and their land was known as "the valley of the carpenters." But they were workers in metals and stone as well as in wood, and they could perform many other services, such as pulling a tooth or mending a broken bone, juggling little balls or playing the flute, singing or anointing, reciting prayers or charming the rains. They would wander from one village to another and perform such services in exchange for food; then they would fill their water skins at the village well and return into the desert, where they hunted small animals with javelins and crooked throw sticks.

When we read about such footloose tribes we think of the gypsies; but the gypsies have a reputation for stealing, whereas the Rechabites and Cainites were religious people with a very strict code. They were Nasoreans, or Nazarites; people who never drank wine, never planted seeds, never looked at a coin, and held a debt sacred. They might be slow in paying; they would wander away, but some day they

13

would return and render a service equal to what had been done for them. They were pacifists in an uncompromising sense; they never harmed any man, and if any harmed them they took it meekly. They avoided being robbed by the device of not having any property of value and letting all men know it. They would help robbers as they helped others, and do so cheerfully, so that the robbers liked them.

By such methods they had managed to survive as free men in a world of slaughter and enslavement. As far back as the days of the Exodus from Egypt, they had "shewed kindness" to the fleeing Israelites; and four centuries later King Saul remembered this and warned them to get out of the way while he was slaughtering the Amalekites; which they did. Three thousand years have passed and they are still doing the same thing. They wander over the deserts of Syria and Arabia, being known as the Slubbim, or Sleb. Travelers have brought accounts of them; they part their hair in the middle, braid it, tie it with a red ribbon, and cover it with turban and neckcloth; they wear long robes of undyed camel's hair, almost touching the ground. They walk barefoot, and the soles of their feet are like deer hide. They still hold themselves apart from all wars; when there is a battle, they stand and watch, and afterwards help the wounded of both sides. If a fugitive comes to them they feed him; if a pursuer comes, they feed him too, but do not tell him which way the fugitive went.

There were many refugees among them; for in the old days the desert was to the Jews what high mountains have been in other lands, the home of freedom. Rebel Jews had a cry, "Shubhu!" which means "Come back"—to us in the wilderness. Criminals came—not always evil men, but offenders against the stern Roman laws. Visionaries came—men who believed that God would speak to them in lonely places, rather than in the wicked towns. Women would come, whose husbands had divorced them and cast them off. Where else could they survive?

The Rechabites were a small people, not over three cubits high, we are told—a cubit being eighteen inches. They were lean and dark-skinned, with long faces and long noses and rather sparse black beards. Despite their smallness they were extremely enduring; they could walk all day in the blazing desert sun; they could do with very little food, and without water for longer than other men. Nature had seen to all that by her age-old implacable method—the weaklings did not survive. So it had been for millennia beyond counting, and so it may be again when the last of the wicked towns has been buried beneath windborne dust.

2

There was one of these Rechabite groups not much bigger than a family; about a dozen adults and as many children. They owned three asses among them, and on these they packed their belongings—food, water, tools and hunting weapons. They had no tents, for in the dry season they needed none, and in the short wet season it was better to seek shelter in some inn where their services were needed, or in the barn of a peasant who knew them of old. Perhaps the pulley over his well had broken and must be repaired; perhaps he had prospered, and wished to have a chest in which to keep his best clothing; perhaps he had tanned the skin of a slaughtered animal and wished it to be cut into a coat or sandals for the family. If the village was small, such skills might be lacking; to say nothing of the healing of wounds and the doctoring of strange diseases of man or beast. In the tribe was an old one named Yonadab the son of Yesse who possessed a little board with a lot of pegs driven into it. At every spare moment he would get this out and practice pulling out the pegs. He had been doing it for most of his life, and as a result he could reach into a man's mouth and extract an aching tooth with one jerk. Such a service was surely worth a night's shelter for the tribe.

One needed strong hands and also sharp wits to survive in this poor man's world. When the tribe came to the Lake of Galilee the fisherman knew them. When they helped to haul in the nets they were awarded a few of the less desirable fishes. When they came to an inn and saw a merchant arriving with a laden ass, they unloaded the goods and carried them into shelter, and so he would invite the men to sup with him and would tell the news from Tyre or Damascus. When they agreed to help load in the morning, he would repay with food for the rest of the family. That would not be begging, but just facing the fact that God had sent children and they had to have the means of life. All good Hebrews understood this.

For the children such a way of life was not without its delights. They saw a great deal of the world, and their days seldom lacked variety. They learned to take care of themselves, and to be useful as soon as they could get about. They

took this for granted, for they had never seen such a thing as
a toy and their play was all preparation for work. They
learned to trap animals in the desert and to catch fish from
the lake or its tributary streams. They learned what plants
had edible roots, and how to start a fire with flints; their
pride was in growing up as quickly as possible and being
helpful to those they loved.

Of the heart's treasures they had an abundance. Their
people were kind by nature and also by creed. Children were
the tribe's future, and were watched over and taught, not
merely how to survive in this world, but how to be taken into
the bosom of the all-good and almighty God who had sent
them. This God had dealt with their forefathers through the
ages; had given them laws which they knew well and feared.
The language they spoke was the Galilean dialect of Aramaic.
Few of them knew its letters, but they knew the proper
prayers to say and the proper hymns to sing when their
prayers were answered; they knew how this great Yahweh, or
Jehovah, had dealt with their forefathers long ago, and what
actions would please Him and what excite His wrath. They
carefully did the former and refrained from the latter, and so
their days remained long in the land which the Lord their
God had given them.

3

In this small Rechabite tribe was a little boy named Yeshu;
his father's name was Yosef and his mother's Marya. The
father was a carpenter, and a good one; a frail man to look
at, but wiry and tough. He had need to be, for the tools he
used were crude and the lumber bulky. He was a pious man,
who put his trust in the Lord and had never been disap-
pointed; he had been blessed with four sons and two daughters, and all of them were living, a rare boon indeed. His
wife was thirty, an advanced age in those days; she was thin,
her face was deeply lined, and the cords stood out in her
neck and wrists. A woman could not foresee when her child
was coming, and it happened often when the tribe was on
the trail. If so, they would wait for her, and she would pick
up the newborn babe and follow along. Some other woman
would offer to carry the burden for a while, and that would
be a favor to be repaid in turn.

Yeshu's early childhood had fallen when there was a
drought and near-famine in the land. Life had been hard, not
merely in the villages, but even in the desert, where more

people came to hunt, and at the lake where they came to fish. Little Yeshu had seldom had enough to eat, and had labored to help his father at heavy tasks. There is some reason to believe that he may have suffered from the disease known to modern science as kyphosis, a distortion of the spine due to malnutrition and overstrain. Carpenters, it appears, are especially liable to it, so much so that German surgeons term it *Schreinerkyphose*. That may have been why in later years Josephus called Yeshu by the Greek word *epíkuphos*, meaning hunchback.

This deformity, lasting through life, may have one of two opposite effects. It may embitter the sufferer and spoil his disposition, or it may cause him to develop his mental powers, and so win the respect of his fellows in spite of an unattractive aspect. It often inclines the victim toward philosophy; we know that it gave the mental stimulus to the Greek Plato, the German Kant, the Jewish Moses Mendelssohn, and Alexander Pope, author of the *Essay on Man*. However it may have been with the desert child, Yeshu ben Yosef, he developed a pair of observant dark eyes, ears that listened attentively, and a mind that laid hold of whatever came within its reach and never let go. He went off and thought about what he had heard, and his thoughts were such that even while he was still a child many recognized him as their mental superior, and marveled at him.

Loving kindness stood first in this lad's nature; and second stood religious faith. The two were really one, for the God of the Rechabites was not Jehovah of the thunders, a God of wrath and vengeance, but One of love and mercy. Evil came somehow, but you did not have to fear it; you only had to love God enough, and He would guide and protect you. He was the Lord of Hosts, the Most High, the God of Abraham, Isaac, and Jacob. He was omnipresent in Yeshu's life and in his thoughts. He sent the sun and rain, He gave food and raiment, He knew everything that a little child had need of. If ever He was busy and overlooked anything, all that was needed was a respectful reminder, and He would hear, and respond if in His judgment it was for the best.

The universe of little Yeshu was small; he had traveled over a small part of it, and heard about the rest. He knew there were great cities such as Damascus and Sidon and Alexandria, that men talked about. He knew that God's Holy Temple was in Jerusalem, and he dreamed of some day making a pilgrimage to it. He knew that the land had been conquered by a haughty people from over the great western sea which we call the Mediterranean, and that they had a capital called Rome. But these people were idol worshipers, and of little interest to a child of the true God, Who had made the world and everything in it, and Who, in His own time, would come again or else send a heavenly Messiah to brush the interlopers out of the way.

Over the earth there stretched an immense dome, a sort of inverted blue bowl. The sun rose at one side and passed overhead and then disappeared; but you didn't have to worry, for God had assigned its course and it always returned at the proper moment. The stars had been set up there to beautify the night, and they behaved in the same way, everything in order. The seasons came, the rains fell and softened the ground, and the seeds sprouted, each according to its own kind. It was the same with all the living creatures which the Almighty One had created in His six days of labor. Every one knew its own food, each grew in its own way, and all served the purposes of man. If there was anything you did not understand, all you had to do was to wait and pray, and in due course God would reveal it to you.

The great God lived high up in the sky, just beyond the blue canopy. Jahweh was his old-time name, but you never dared to speak it; He was Adonai, the Lord. He sent the thunder, to remind frail man of His power. Since He had made man in His own image, it was obvious that He must look like a man; an elderly Big Man with a benevolent aspect and a wonderful black beard. In old times He had come down and revealed Himself to great men like Moses. More often He sent a messenger, called an angel of the Lord. Or He sent prophets, inspired teachers, who spoke to the people; but that had not happened for many generations now. It might be that He was displeased with his chosen people. "We must learn to pray harder," said Yeshu's father, and the other men of the tribe agreed; also pious ones, the Zealots who came visiting in the deserts, and wise ones who lived in the villages on the tribe's rounds. A stream of prayers must ascend to the Lord God of Israel, the God of Gods, the Lord of Hosts. It was a kind of moral pressure that was put upon Him, and He could not indefinitely resist. Great as He was, He had need of His children's affection, such being the nature of love.

4

It is a mistake to think that because people do not know their letters they must be ignorant about the important things of life. They can carry a library about in their heads, and hand it on to their children and their children's children. This little tribe of ragged desert people knew by heart some of the world's great literature, and in them were the seeds of many cultures. They could not see the future, but they knew the past, and because of it they walked with honorable pride.

Seated around their campfire at night, with jackals barking nearby, old Yonadab the wheelwright who pulled teeth and Ya'acob the smith who danced before the Lord told wonder stories about this Almighty One who had created the world in six days. Stage by stage He had done it, and had revealed the process. He had created a man, and then, seeing that He was lonely, had taken a rib from his body and made it into a woman. He had set them in a wonderful garden full of all the fruits—a gift these poorly-nourished persons knew how to appreciate. The serpent had come in—and how well these barefooted ones knew him and his treacherous ways! He had tempted Eve to eat the forbidden apple, and so the pair had been expelled from the Garden of Eden, and they and their seed had ever since been forced to earn their bread by the sweat of their faces.

Much later, for their sins, Yahweh permitted them to be enslaved by the Egyptians; then, because of their prayers, He raised up Moses, and sent a series of plagues to torment the Egyptians until they let the Israelites go. The Egyptians pursued them, and the Lord opened a path through the Red Sea; the chosen people marched through it, but when their enemies tried to follow, the Lord let the waters loose and they were all drowned. Could one imagine a story more thrilling to the soul of a child like this, sitting by a campfire with the stars shining over his head and the jackals lurking just beyond the firelight?

And the story of the vast migration, seeking for the promised land! It was in a wilderness of the south, the Arabian peninsula, rocky and barren like Transjordan, but even hotter. For forty years the Israelites wandered, and Yahweh went before them as a pillar of cloud by day and a pillar of fire by night; when water failed He told Moses to smite a rock with his staff, and when food failed He dropped manna from heaven. How nice if He would do that now for the

Rechabites! That He didn't could only be because they did not make themselves worthy; little Yeshu resolved that he would pray harder, and persuade his brothers and sisters to join with him—for it was well known that prayers are more effective when two or three are gathered together.

In the Exodus from Egypt there were six hundred thousand fighting men, and with their wives and children the total must have been two million. To a little boy this figure meant nothing, for never in his life had he seen a thousand people together. But when they told him about the Tabernacle in the Wilderness, he could know about that, for he was a carpenter's son, and learning to be a carpenter himself, and tradition gave the dimensions of this marvelous structure. It could be dismantled and carried about, and took twenty-two thousand of the sons of Levi to act as porters.

Oriental religious buildings face the east, in order to catch the first rays of the rising sun; but it never occurred to little Yeshu that this might have been because his people had originally been sun-worshipers. "On the east side, toward the rising of the sun, shall they of the standard of the camp of Judah pitch"—so ran the command, and the child was thrilled when he heard it, because as a son of David he was of that tribe which had the position of honor. But he repressed the feeling, for it was his duty to love all men, and pride was permitted only to Yahweh, who was a jealous God. Pride in the Tabernacle was different, because that had been made at the Terrible One's command; to Yeshu this gold-studded structure was just as real as the rocks against which now and then he stubbed his bare toes. He saw it in the distance, shining in the rays of every morning sun; he saw its hosts advancing with banners, the faithful porters carrying the numbered sections, and the swordsmen and archers surrounding them to guard the precious burden.

5

Throughout their long history these Israelites had lived surrounded by other kinds of people, all of whom worshiped strange gods; and always the Israelites were under temptation by these more pleasure-loving deities, male and female. Always there were prophets arising, storming at the false gods; these beings existed, one gathered from the prophets, but they were demons, and all the misfortunes that ever befell the chosen people were because they had weakened in their faith and taken up the practices of their enemies. Baal and

Beelzebub and Moloch and Ashtaroth, gods of Philistines and Phoenicians and Babylonians and Hittites and Jebusites and Amorites—the ancient records are full of their names. Because of this wickedness, the Lord their God permitted King Nebuchadnezzar from Babylon to conquer His people and destroy His Temple; the Israelites were carried off into captivity, and remained in that state for nearly a century, a terrible experience. Their priests and leaders learned the bitter lesson, and when at last Adonai, the Lord, had caused the Babylonians to release them, the Israelite scholars set to work to compose history and propaganda which should teach the chosen people to fear their Lord and Master, and never again to forget the strict monotheism which He required of them.

Again they were conquered, by Alexander of Macedon, and then by the Syrians; but they managed to hold on to their faith, and in the end to rise and rebel. Now they were subjects of the masterful Romans; and this time it was less hard, because the conquerors, having many gods of their own, were easy-going, and allowed all the strange tribes to worship as they pleased, provided they paid their taxes and obeyed the Roman law. These conquerors even let the Hebrews have a king of their own, a puppet king selected for them. The Romans were men of this world, rulers and money-makers, who had learned to smile over the superstitions of their own forefathers, as well as those of the lesser breeds.

Such was the world into which Yeshu was born; but he knew little about it and cared less. He had his God, who was the true God, Elohim, in whom he lived and moved and had his being. The Romans had this world, but could keep it only so long as the Lord of Hosts saw fit to let them. A passionate monotheism was the very core of little Yeshu's being; he loved the Lord, and contemplated with horror the idea that there could be any other Lord, or anyone who shared the Lord's power. The child could recite, and frequently did, the ten commandments which the Lord had handed to Moses, engraved upon tablets of stone. The first of these commandments read: "I am the Lord thy God, which have brought thee out of the land of Egypt, out of the house of bondage. Thou shalt not make unto thee any graven image, or any likeness of anything that is in heaven above, or that is in the earth beneath, or in the waters under the earth. Thou shalt not bow thyself down to them, nor serve them: for I, the Lord thy God, am a jealous God, visiting the iniquity of the fathers upon the children unto the third and fourth generation of them that hate me, and showing mercy unto thousands of them that love me, and kept my commandments." Little Yeshu took this stern word so literally that he would not, as children love to do, make any play image out of clay, or scratch a picture of anything in the desert sand. When the Lord thy God gives thee an order, He means exactly what He says, and no less. He is a stern God, and has told you to fear Him.

The little boy heard talk about the Roman gods, many of whose statues stood in the government city of Tiberias, on the far shore of the lake. There was a head god named Jupiter, and he had a wife, but was not faithful to her; he sometimes came down to earth and cohabited with a woman and made her pregnant. So there were demigods, sons and daughters of gods; and as the desert child grew older and thought about it, that seemed to him the most abhorrent idea in all the world. Of course there was a sense in which we were all children of God; but that was a different thing, that was in a spiritual sense, and did not alter the fact that God was God and men were men, and all men were equals in the sight of God and should be in the sight of one another. To say that one man could be God or that a God could be born of a woman was the very essence of idol-worship, it was the 'iniquity' referred to in the First Commandment.

6

When Yeshu was twelve years old there befell a great adventure in his life; the tribe decided to travel to Jerusalem for the Passover. This was the most important festival of the Hebrews, dating from the days of their captivity in Egypt. As a final and supreme miracle to obtain their freedom Yahweh had sent His angel to destroy the eldest son in each of the Egyptian families. The Israelites were instructed to make a mark of lamb's blood upon the doors of their houses, so that the destroying angel would pass over them; hence the name of the festival. Naturally the Israelites appreciated this favor, and every spring they came to the Temple and there sacrificed the Paschal lamb and ate its flesh.

Yeshu's tribe talked about what they were going to see, and a little boy listened with wide open ears. Jerusalem was to him the handiwork of the Lord; its Temple—the only one permitted in all Israel—had been built according to His precise instructions, and was a place of wonder, full of gold and jewels. Seventy-five thousand persons inhabited Jerusalem in those days—which does not make a great city according to modern standards, but it was vast indeed to a desert child. How many pilgrims would come was beyond estimate. The roads would be thronged with them, some walking, some riding on asses, all leading the choice animals they brought as sacrifices to the Most Holy Lord. It must have been the greatest spectacle of those days.

This Temple had been built first by Solomon, the greatest king the Jews had ever had. His wealth and power could be realized from the fact that he had had a thousand wives— one wife being a luxury which many men could not afford. The Temple had been destroyed by King Nebuchadnezzar —and what terrible stories the tribe had to tell about *him!* He had carried away all the treasures of the king's house, and the treasures of the house of the Lord, including the vessels of gold and the jewels. He had carried away the princes and the men of valor, the wives of the king, his officers, and all the mighty of the land. He had left only the poor, "to be vine dressers and husbandmen." He reigned in Babylon in his pride and glory, but the Lord sent him bad dreams, and he had to have the Israelite prophet Daniel to interpret his dreams and tell him what they meant. He set up a golden image, and for that the Lord sent him warnings of dreadful things, and they all came about. "He was driven from men, and did eat grass as oxen, and his body was wet with the dew of Heaven, till his hair was grown like eagle's feathers, and his nails like bird's claws." Surely a lesson for idol worshipers, and little Yeshu learned it once for all.

There was a great deal of jesting in the tribe, because Yosef had a nephew who was at the proper age for marriage, and it was a tradition in Jerusalem and throughout that portion of the Israelite land called Judea that Rechabites married the daughters of priests. No doubt the custom had originated in the old days when priests were poor like other men, and may have had trouble in finding proper husbands for their daughters; but now priests were gentlemen, many possessing tracts of land and slaves. The tradition must have been embarrassing to them—but still, no tradition could be neglected. When wild men came in from the desert, needing to have their hair cut and finger nails cleaned, the priests had to face the fact that the visitors were sons of David.

In those days it was the custom for the Israelites to sell their daughters. The transaction wasn't called by that impolite name, but the husbands paid a marriage portion and a regular contract was drawn up. However, as the priests had become rich they no longer needed the money, and also it became difficult to find young men who had the money. There had been invented a device by which the bridegroom paid a token portion, and the contract provided that the rest need be paid only if he should divorce the wife and send her back into her father's keeping. So poor men came up to Jerusalem, hoping to find wives on the basis of their distinguished ancestry. The desert people regarded this as a sort of betrayal of the tribe, which needed its able-bodied members; on the other hand, it was a temptation to young men who could never hope to earn a marriage portion. The poor man of those days had a hard life, and it needed a true saint to resist the idea of being taken into the home of a well-to-do priest.

Through the ages there has existed a conflict both economic and cultural between the people of the town and those of the country. The town exploits the country, or so the country people feel. They have to take their products to town and compete with one another in marketing. The townspeople do not compete so freely, but frequently got together to hold up prices. Without the country people they would not have food; but somehow they grow fat and clothe themselves in fine raiment. Also they get learning, and what they call manners, and they look down on the country people, calling them contemptuous names. The Aramaic phrase was *'am ha-aretz,* that is, people of the soil; but it had come to have a contemptuous meaning, like the words we use in our land, 'hicks' and 'hayseeds' and 'hillbillies.' The hill lands of Galilee had few towns, so their people were looked down upon by the people of rich Judea in the south. The Galileans in turn looked down upon the desert people and thought of them as we think of vagabonds—disregarding the fact that they were living strictly in accordance with the traditions of the early Israelites. Moveover, half the Galileans were gentiles, and so when Yeshu came into a town it was as into a foreign land.

7

Palestine is a small country, an area about the size of the state of Vermont and of somewhat the same shape, smaller from east to west and longer from north to south. The distance from the Lake of Galilee to Jerusalem is about seventy-five miles, and at the rate the tribe traveled it should have taken them a week. But they did not go directly, for there was never any hurry in their lives, and they had learned by experience about travel conditions at the time of the Passover. There would be hordes of people coming from every direction, and having their beasts and their carts. All the inns and sleeping places would be crowded. The prices of food would greatly increase—for human nature, alas, has much evil in it, and there were persons, even Hebrews, who were not above taking advantage of the pilgrims coming to the sacrifice. The pilgrims would be in a hurry to get to their destination before their money ran out. They would have little use for the services of Rechabites, and would put these in the position of beggars.

The thing to do was to travel by their old desert routes where they knew the scattered wells and could hunt their food. They would go eastward into the land of the Syrians and down through Transjordan, and take a month or two for the journey. Yeshu was so excited over the idea of seeing the Holy Temple that he walked on air instead of the rough desert floor, and there went before him a pillar of cloud by day and a pillar of fire by night. He plied the members of his family and the rest of the tribe with questions, and talked incessantly about what they told him.

He did his best to remember all the obligations which the Law laid upon him, in order that he might be fit in the sight of the Lord. When they came to a well he took water and went apart and washed himself carefully. When there was no well and no water to be spared he would find a stretch of clean sand, and take some of it and rub his body with that. The Law required that he wash his hands before eating, and every member of the tribe was careful to do that, even though the washing had to be symbolical, with two or three drops of the precious fluid on the hands. Also, when a member of the tribe went apart to ease himself he always took along a paddle of wood or bit of brushwood and scraped a hole in the ground, in order to cover that which came from him. As the Holy Word told him, "The Lord thy God walketh in the

midst of thy camp to deliver thee, and to give up thine
enemies before thee; therefore shall thy camp be holy: that
He see no unclean thing in thee and turn away from thee."

Yeshu's Lord was not going to turn away from him. Every
night before going to sleep he went out among the jackals—
they were cowardly beasts and no man need fear them, but
helpless creatures, such as babies, had to be protected from
them. Yeshu would stand on the desert floor—he had never
heard of such a practice as kneeling down to pray. He raised
his hands to the sky where he knew the Lord was, and recited the prayers he had been taught, prayers for protection
and for the needs of life, but most of all prayers that his
heart might be kept pure so that he might be worthy of the
presence of the Lord. Some of these prayers were in the
ancient Hebrew, a language the chosen people had forgotten,
and which learned ones preserved for use in the Temple and
the synagogues. Little Yeshu had learned prayers in Hebrew
and what they meant.

It is a grand sonorous language and lends itself excellently
to chanting. It is poetry but has no rhymes. The verse-form
consists in the saying of the same thing twice over in a different set of phrases, and the one who chants sways his body
from side to side in accord with the rhythm. Any physical
defects of Yeshu did not trouble him, and surely would not
trouble the Lord who had seen fit to send him afflictions, perhaps in order to save him from the sin of pride. Yeshu prayed
to have his heart clean, and to have his people preserved in
the favor of the Lord and made worthy of that mercy. He
stood in the starlight with the wild creatures prowling about,
and he did not fear anything because he knew that he was
safe in the Lord's keeping. He prayed aloud but not in a loud
voice, for that was unnecessary; the Lord was here and everywhere, and heard all voices and even knew all thoughts.
Yeshu chanted the sacred words of his great ancestor King
David, who also had gone apart into the wilderness of Judea:

"O God, Thou art my God; early will I seek Thee; my soul
thirsteth for Thee, my flesh longeth for Thee in a dry and
thirsty land, where no water is; to see Thy power and Thy
glory, so as I have seen Thee in the sanctuary. Because Thy
lovingkindness is better than life, my lips shall praise Thee.
Thus will I bless Thee while I live; I will lift up my hands in
Thy name. My soul shall be satisfied as with marrow and fat-
ness; and my mouth shall praise Thee with joyful lips: when
I remember Thee upon my bed, and meditate on Thee in the

night watches. Because Thou hast been my help, therefore in
the shadow of Thy wings will I rejoice. My soul followeth
hard after Thee: Thy right hand upholdeth me."

8

Yeshu's tribe came within sight of Mt. Nebo, a holy sight
because it was there that the Lord told Moses to go and die;
and Moses went there and died and was buried. That was the
ancient land of Moab, but there were no Moabites now, only
humble desert people like the Rechabites and Cainites. Turning west they came to the river Jordan, near where it flows
into the Dead Sea. There was a ferry, a broad and solidly
built boat upon which even a chariot could be carried across,
with the horses unharnessed and swimming behind. The pilgrims did not know how to swim, and their asses were heavily
laden. They bargained with the ferrymen, and when these
learned that the desert pilgrims had no money they offered
to take them across as a service to the Lord. But to this the
Rechabites would not hear, and pledged themselves that
when they came back they would bring some food which
they would earn by their labors; or perhaps there would be
need of repairs to this boat, or to the mud hut in which the
ferrymen lived.

The boat was propelled by long sweeps, and the passengers
laid on to these right heartily under the direction of the
master, so he and his helper did not have to work but only to
watch. The whole company was safely put across in one
load, and when they were on the far bank, they did not fail
to stand and give thanks to the Lord in a psalm which they
sang in harmony and by which the ferrymen were greatly
edified.

"Oh that men would praise the Lord for His goodness, and
for His wonderful works to the children of men! And let
them sacrifice the sacrifices of thanksgiving, and declare His
works with rejoicing. They that go down to the sea in ships,
that do business in great waters; these see the works of the
Lord, and His wonders in the deep. For He commandeth, and
raiseth the stormy wind, which lifteth up the waves thereof.
They mount up to the heaven, they go down again to the
depths their soul is melted because of trouble. They reel to
and fro, and stagger like a drunken man, and are at their
wit's end. Then they cry unto the Lord in their trouble, and
He bringeth them out of their distresses. He maketh the
storm a calm, so that the waves thereof are still. Then are

they glad because they be quiet; so He bringeth them unto their desired haven. Of that men would praise the Lord for His goodness, and for His wonderful works to the children of men!"

It was true that no such perils had been encountered on the voyage across a small, slow river, but it pleased the ferrymen to imagine that it might have been so. They saw that their voyagers were indeed God-minded people in spite of their low worldly condition, and they assured the voyagers that the concert they had provided was ample compensation for the services, and that they were to consider themselves under no further obligation.

9

The Romans were great road builders. They had to transport armies from one province to another, and their officials and business men desired to travel in comfort. In front of the travelers was the city of Jericho, and from there to Jerusalem was a paved highway; but the desert people did not travel upon it, for it was crowded, and the stones of the pavement were hard upon the feet. The Rechabites, as was their custom, sought out the bypaths and the places where poor people made their homes. In the presence of such people they were not ashamed, and the humble food which these people provided was sufficient. There was work for carpenters and smiths, to say nothing of doctors and dentists, chanters of hymns and diviners of the future.

A little boy had his duties assigned. He would help to unload the asses, and then he would lead them out to where there was pasture on the mountain side; he would hobble them with cords so that they could not wander too far, and then he would sit and watch. This left him plenty of time to look at the land of Judea, new and strange to him. It lay further to the south and was warmer. Now in the springtime there were showers, and the boy would find what shelter he could under a tree. He had been taught to look upon the rain as something precious, a gift from the Lord in a thirsty land. It was the promised land which the Lord had given to the children of Israel, and they had come into it rejoicing and singing after forty years of wandering in the wilderness. In the soul of this desert child the drama of seventeen centuries earlier was repeated, and the joys and thanksgivings of all the two million Israelite immigrants were revived and concentrated in his soul.

Ahead of them lay the Holy City, and now that it was
no longer possible to avoid the throngs of people who were
crowding into it this little tribe of desert people would have
to survive on what food they had brought, and what might be
given them for that charity which is enjoined upon Hebrews.
In old days, when the Israelites had been a pastoral people,
the sacrifice of a ceremonial lamb had involved no hard-
ship; but with wandering artisans it was a different matter.
They would have to earn the price, and find others to share
the cost. It must be a he-lamb of the first year, and without
blemish. It must be killed on the evening before the Passover,
and according to the ritual completely drained of blood.
Then it must be roasted and eaten entire by the Israelites,
and there must be no stranger or uncircumcized person present at the feast. It must be on the fifteenth of the month
Nisan, and for seven days thereafter the observers of the
festival must eat only the mazzoth, the unleavened bread.

How all these details of ritual originated is a matter about
which learned scholars have been disputing for many, many
years. But little Yeshu knew nothing about that, he only knew
that it was according to the orders of the Lord, and must be
obeyed with strictness and at the same time with joy, for it
was a festival of freedom. The celebrants must be ready with
loins girded, shoes on feet and staff in hand, as if prepared
for a journey, as their ancestors had been. This, of course,
was easy for the Rechabites and seemed perfectly natural and
proper.

10

The Holy City stood upon a group of hills, and the Temple
stood upon the highest of these. It had been completely
destroyed by the Babylonians, but recently King Herod had
rebuilt it. It was the pleasure of these ancient rulers to tax
the people heavily, and spend the money upon magnificent
buildings which would cause the ruler's name to be remembered by future ages. During the thirty-three years of Herod's
reign he had made a new Temple, much larger, much hand-
somer, and with twice the space in its outer courts. The
structure was partly a place of sacrifice and worship, and
partly a fortress. Its walls were built for defense, and its en-
trances were narrow and provided with heavy gates.

The city also had walls, and many gates through which the
traffic of the countryside came in. There was a west hill
which was high, and had cool breezes; here the rich and ele-

gant had their dwellings. On the other small hills and in the valleys between lived the artisans, shopkeepers, and other plebeians. The crowding was beyond anything that modern people could imagine. Whole families lived in a room smaller than ten feet square, and the streets and alleys were so narrow that a laden ass could hardly get through. There had been lawsuits because of the fact that an ass with a load of flax on its back had been set fire to by a candle burning in a merchant's doorway. To people used to the wide open spaces of the desert the confusion and uproar were paralyzing; they knew not which way to turn and had a hard time keeping together. All the pilgrims crowded into the great outer court of the Temple, because there was no other place for them. Here they ate, here they slept, and if it rained they and their beasts cowered and took it as best they could. There was no shelter.

Following closely in the wake of his father, little Yeshu stared at the sights of this tremendous city. They wandered through the alleys, gazing at the variety of goods which merchants in little booths set out for sale. Customers would stop, and chaffering would begin, rising to a clamor after the fashion of oriental lands. Here was the unleavened bread of the Passover, baked in large round flat discs. Here were turnips, garlic and cabbages, the food of the poor. Here were articles of clothing, pottery of many designs, and the few crude tools of that time. Because Yeshu's father had no money, he could only look. He could listen to the talk of the people, much of it incomprehensible—Latin, Greek, even Persian and Egyptian. Merchants had come by camel train across the deserts and by ships on the sea. There was money to be made here at the festival time, and all the world had known the fact.

The desert child never climbed the hill where the rich lived. He knew there was nothing for him up there, and he could look at the beautiful buildings from a distance. The greatest of all was the palace which had been built by King Herod, and was now occupied by his successor. There had been an uprising against the government in the previous year, and the porticos of the palace had been burned. Yeshu had heard about this at the time.

What went on in those palaces was not unknown to the poor, for the literature of the Israelites was full of social protest; the ways of the rich were stormed at in extravagant but eloquent detail, and Yeshu knew some of these passages by

heart. Here in the bazaars it was easy to engage people in
talk, and they would tell all about the patricians of the city
and in what pride they walked. They held themselves so far
aloof from the poor that they would not sign a legal document unless they knew who the other witnesses were; they
would not sit in judgment unless they knew who the other
judges were, nor accept an invitation to dinner unless they
knew who else was to be present. You would hear talk about
how, when they carried palm branches in the ceremonies of
the Sukkot week, they would have to have these branches
fixed with bindings of real gold. In the same way their
phylacteries had to be covered with gold. There was a story
of a rich lady who had bought the high priesthood for her
husband; wishing to attend the service of the Day of Atone-
ment where it was forbidden to wear shoes, and being un-
willing to have her delicate feet touch the earth, she had
had coverings of silk spread on the street, all the way from
her dwelling-place to the Temple mount. Such people were
so proud of themselves, they had altogether forgotten the
Lord. "Hear ye, and give ear; be not proud: for the Lord
hath spoken."

11

Strange races and strange costumes and strange tongues
could not fail to fascinate a boy of twelve; but most of all he
was interested in the Temple, the wonderful structure of his
dreams, more magnificent than any desert dream could have
been. It had been enormously costly, having a great inner
court with the altar upon which the sacrifices were burned.
Here bullocks and sheep were brought and it was like a
slaughter house; but there was nothing about this to shock
an Israelite lad, who was used to seeing animals killed, and
to helping dress them. Besides, it was done here in the name
of the Lord and at His command.

In the Temple itself, the Holy Place, was a sight for which
he had not been prepared. In the old days the Israelites had
had bullocks, rams and lambs of their own, and could bring
them as sacrifices to the Lord, and as food for His holy
priests; but now many of the Israelites were artisans settled
in towns, or merchants and traders. For the sacrifice they had
to buy animals, and that meant that there had developed a
great business of shipping these creatures and marketing them
in the Temple courts. The place had become a stockyards,
with bellowing and bleating and no end of unpleasant odors.

These creatures were sold for money, and men had brought them there, not to the glory of God, but to their selfish profit; worse yet, the moneychangers had set up their tables in the Temple itself. There had to be such conveniences, for many kinds of people had many kinds of money. A peasant of Judea who had brought in half a dozen of his sheep did not want to take home the Greek drachma or the Roman denarius or the Persian daric. He wanted the shekels of his own district, so the pilgrim who wanted to buy a lamb had to go to the money-changers, who would offer him a price for his coins. If he thought it was not enough, he would go to the next moneychanger, and they would wrangle and perhaps lose their tempers and scream at each other, and so the place became a babel, and the sight was most unpleasant to a worshipful soul who had come expecting an atmosphere of reverence and awe.

Up behind the Ark of the Covenant was the Holy of Holies behind a curtain. No one dared lift that curtain; if he had done so, he would have found nothing there, which symbolized the fact that the Jews worshiped no idol, but worshiped God in the spirit. But what sort of spirit would consent to dwell in a place that rang with the shouts of men disputing over the value of gold and silver and copper discs with the images of heathen rulers on them? "O God, the heathen are come into thine inheritance; Thy Holy temple have they defiled." So had spoken the glorious King David, forefather of little Yeshu, and Yeshu had heard his words.

12

The tribe had made a few pairs of sandals, and they now exchanged some of these for a share in a Paschal he-lamb of the first year and without blemish. This was slaughtered on the afternoon of the fourteenth day, and in the evening it was cooked and eaten with proper pious enjoyment. But the tribe could not stay for the full twenty-one days of the festival; they had no such supply of food, and it was difficult to earn it in a city where unemployment was prevalent and the wages of an artisan were no more than one dinar, or twenty-five cents a day.

They decided to leave suddenly, in the company of some Rechabite friends they had met. There was quite a throng, and in the confusion of departure little Yeshu was missing. He had gone wandering to gaze at the activities of the priests. When he came back to the place in the outer court he found his family gone. He made inquiry, but no one knew anything except that they had loaded up their asses and disappeared. He spent the rest of the day wandering and searching but without success. He did not worry too much, for he was sure that the Lord God of Israel would take care of him.

When evening came he was hungry. The piece of unleavened bread and the half-dozen dried olives which he had eaten during the day had not lasted long in a boy's stomach. He did not wish to beg, and looked about to find some way to make himself useful. He picked out one of the Temple force of workers, an elderly man with a kind face, wearing the uniform of the gatekeepers. He approached this man and asked if perchance there was any provision in the Temple affairs for lost children. It was an accident which happened often in this throng, but it was left to charity and the mercy of God.

The gatekeeper talked with this frail little boy with the well-worn camel's coat, obviously from one of the desert tribes, and by his accent a Galilean, one of the despised *'am ha-aretz*. "I will take care of you for the night, my son," said the man, and this was indeed a wonderful adventure for little Yeshu, who stood in awe of the humblest official in this wondrous institution. A Levite he was, a separate tribe or caste set apart for the service of the Lord. They had been in this service for several hundred years, and their jobs were handed down from father to son, an hereditary privilege. They lived within the Temple precincts, and the old man took the boy to his home, a small and crowded room, but no less wonderful to Yeshu for that.

The Levite family were pious folk and did not look down upon a ragged desert child. He belonged to the Lord, and to show him charity was a worthy work in the Lord's sight. They gave him a share of unleavened bread, and herbs cooked with olive oil. It was all that Yeshu expected, and he appreciated the charity given in the sacred Name. "For the Lord your God is God of gods,"—so ran the injunction—"and Lord of lords, a great God, a mighty, and a terrible, which regardeth not persons, nor taketh reward: He doth execute the judgment of the fatherless and widow, and loveth the stranger, in giving him food and raiment. Love ye therefore the stranger: for ye were strangers in the land of Egypt."

13

This servant of the Lord must have been impressed by the mental powers of the child he had picked up, for he sat until late in the evening talking, and telling the inside affairs of the wonderful Temple. The Levite, it developed, was dissatisfied with his lot in life, and found the service of the Lord less honorable than it was supposed to be. In the first place the people throughout the whole of the land of Israel failed to pay their tithes according to the sacred Law. They were supposed to bring a tenth of all the fruits of the land for the service of the Lord, and to deliver them in Jerusalem; but they often did not trouble to come at all. There was supposed to be a second tithe which they themselves would consume in Jerusalem. That would mean new business in the Holy City, and more money spent in the Temple; but alas, they did not bother with either kind of tithe. They said it was too far, the journey too difficult, and they had their hands full taking care of their flocks, their harvests, and their possessions. No longer were they the simple pastoral people who could travel from one place to another, driving their herds along. Now they were settled, and some had grown too rich, and others were too poor, earning only enough each day to keep them alive the next.

Also, the Levites were collectively unhappy because of their struggle with the priests. Under the old Law they were servants of the Lord and of His Holy Temple; but the priests tried to make out that the Levites were servants of the priests, and the proud ones were always pushing to degrade them to that position. There had been going on a little war ever since the Restoration, five hundred years ago. The hereditary priesthood had become wealthy; they had forgotten knowledge and the service of the Lord; they neglected their duties, they walked haughtily, they dressed themselves in fine raiment, and associated only with the aristocracy. They were often ignorant and boorish, their manners were bad, they looked down upon their servants, or those whom they wished to consider their servants. Here in the Temple they kept elaborate genealogical records, and knew who everybody was, and who his forefathers were, and they would associate only with the sons of David. Yehoiarib—that was the name of this gatetender—was greatly impressed when little Yeshu told him that he was a son of David, and Yehoiarib said that he would look it up in the records in the morning.

Moreover there were quarrels among the Levites themselves; they, too, were divided into castes and warring groups. There were the sacred singers, who made pretension to importance, but knew only the music which they sang. The gate-keepers, on the other hand, had leisure, and many were students and scholars. Yehoiarib could read words, and not just music. Yehoiarib had made use of the Temple library; he knew the Torah, the sacred Law, and knew his rights under that Law; but, alas, it was hard to protect his rights, because he was a poor man, and the wage he received was barely enough to keep his family alive. The Law was supposed to cover everything for a Jew, business and politics, manners and morals; but more and more it was being neglected, and the rich and powerful were making friends with the Romans, and even admiring the culture of the degenerate Greeks.

All this surprised Yeshu greatly. He had taken for granted that the Holy Temple must be full of the spirit of the Lord, and that all who served it must live in a state of exaltation. "I will praise the Lord with my whole heart, in the assembly of the upright, and in the congregation." But instead there was wrangling, jealousy, and greed. Little Yeshu from the desert was greatly shocked, and lay awake thinking over this night's conversation. He remembered the prophet Micah: "They build up Zion with blood, and Jerusalem with iniquity. The heads thereof judge for reward, and the priests thereof teach for hire, and the prophets thereof divine for money: yet will they lean upon the Lord, and say, Is not the Lord among us? none evil can come upon us. Therefore shall Zion for your sake be plowed as a field, and Jerusalem shall become heaps, and the mountain of the house as the high places of the forest."

14

Yeshu slept in the corner of the crowded room on a sheep pelt, with another to cover him from the chill of the night. That was perfect comfort, and if fleas bit him, that was according to expectation. There were fleas even in the Holy Temple—how could it be otherwise, with herds of beasts being brought in every day? Yeshu had never known what it was to sleep in a room without fleas; they were one of the reasons for preferring the desert. While he lay awake and worried about the state of Israel in its dealings with the Lord, he listened to the lowing of the doomed cattle and the bleating of the doomed sheep, and it seemed to him that Israel was like unto them and should be spending the night crying to the Lord for deliverance from its sins. But the rest of the family slept and snored heartily, and at last Yeshu slept also.

He was awakened with the dawn, and performed his ablution behind a screen—there was water in the Temple, and for all the well-to-do in Jerusalem, brought by an aqueduct from the distant hills. The visitor breakfasted on unleavened bread and dried olives, the staple food of the poor. He was given a couple of dried figs because he was a guest, and a worthy one. Then he accompanied his host to the Temple services. He listened to the chanting, watched the sacrifices, and was shown the Temple library with its precious scrolls. The books of those days were written by hand on parchment, and this parchment was rolled into bulky scrolls which were kept each in a box called a *capsa* and never touched save by those who had authority. The only private persons who could own them were the very rich—who as a rule had no time to bother with them. To little Yeshu it appeared that a man who had his food and shelter provided, and who had been able to learn to read, and was permitted to take one of these scrolls and study it—such a man ought to be completely contented with his lot in life.

Yehoiarib was kind, and evidently had been greatly impressed by this prematurely wise little boy, for he went off and brought one of the scribes of the Temple, a learned doctor. This black-bearded one seated himself by Yeshu and entered into conversation. He questioned the lad about his life and his ideas, and when he realized what a gentle and worshipful little son of David this was, in spite of his unpromising costume and physique, he went off and brought others of his associates. They were all venerable and impressive in appearance—and Yeshu was duly impressed. They wore white linen sheets with fringes—which meant they were Pharisees.

The order of the Pharisees had been formed a century or more before for the purpose of preserving the laws of Levitical purity. They knew both the Law and the Prophets pretty well by heart, and spent their time disputing about the fine points of doctrine and ritual. They were never more delighted than when they could trip one another up, or trip up some stranger and show how he, perhaps without realizing it, was putting the future of his soul in peril. Their speech was so elegant that sometimes the lad from the desert had difficulty in understanding what they were saying. He was enormously impressed by their long black beards, and still more by those that were gray. Above all things he had been taught to venerate age, whether it was in a man, or a book, or a Temple, or the great Adonai who had made them all.

They asked Yeshu about his family, and their life as desert wanderers. By tradition they respected this life, because it had been the life of their forefathers. No Israelite had forgotten, or ever would forget, those forty years of wandering, and all the laws and regulations which God had given to Moses, and which Moses had handed on to his people. How well did these modern wanderers keep the ordinances? The learned doctors inquired, and Yeshu told them all that he knew, soberly and earnestly. Yes, they all carried a paddle wherewith to bury in the desert that which came from their bodies. Yes, they all wore phylacteries, and they had sacred words written in them—at least, they had been told they were sacred words, but, alas, they could not read them. As for door-post inscriptions—well, what could desert people do about that? They had no door posts and no doors, but when they came to the doors of other persons, then, of course, they were glad to see the inscriptions and to have the meanings told to them.

The naive little visitor was distressed to learn that these dignified and learned gentlemen looked down upon the Galileans, not merely because of their accent, but because they did not rigidly obey the Jewish laws of cleanliness, and, therefore, were impure and unfit to be associated with. What, for example, did they do about the ashes of a red heifer? Alas, little Yeshu had never even heard about this, and it had to be told to him. Jewish Law considered anyone impure who had touched a corpse, and he had to wait apart from his fellows for seven days, and then had to be purified by a special ceremony which included being washed with water mixed with the ashes of a red heifer. These ashes were infinitely precious and sacred. The heifer had to be one that had not so much as a single black hair in his coat, and after it had been ceremonially killed and ceremonially burned its ashes were preserved in the Temple and used in the ceremony of purification. But what could poor people in the desert do about a thing like that? They never even so much as saw a heifer; at least not until they came into the village of Galilee, and little Yeshu had to admit that he had never seen an entirely red heifer in his life. But he had seen people die and seen them buried, with a pile of stones put over the bodies, and he had never known that his fellow tribesmen were impure because they had performed this action.

There were so many traps for the feet of the unwary! Many Hebrews, it appeared, were going about with the curse of the Lord God upon them, and without having any idea of it. In the course of his talk Yeshu referred to the practice of irrigating land—very common throughout Palestine. There were two kinds of land; that which had been irrigated, and that which had been naturally watered. The country people of Galilee had a phrase for a field that was watered by rain—they called it Bet-ha-Baal. Now he learned that this phrase had come down from the old days, when the people of that land had worshiped a local deity called Baal, who was to be supposed to bring rain and protect the fertility of the soil. For the first time in his life little Yeshu learned that the phrase he had spoken was an evil idolatrous one, which should never pass the lips of a proper monotheistic Israelite. In fact the Pharisees had a rule that they never even spoke the name of Baal; all they would say was Boshet, which meant shame. Yeshu thought this was an excellent idea, and promised to make it known to his people, and to adopt the practice himself.

15

One of the learned gentlemen whom the guest met during these unforgettable days was a Sadducee. This was a still more strictly pious sect; they quarreled with the Pharisees, accusing them of laxity in this and that. The Sadducees did not wear fringes, and did not believe in the resurrection of the body, calling it a Persian and Egyptian notion.

This learned one was ill-pleased with Yeshu, and informed him that all Galileans were hopelessly impure forever; they were a crude and ignorant people, half-gentile and wholly outside the province of the Law. For example, it was well-known that they washed olives; but every proper Jew knew that when olives were touched with any sort of moisture after being plucked, they became impure and it was a sin to eat them. No, little Yeshu had never heard this; he promised to obey the Law in the future, and the Sadducee commanded him to learn the passage and repeat it after him. Yeshu repeated it word for word, and as it was a long passage this was considered quite a feat.

The Sadducee remarked, with sarcasm in his voice, "You must be very proud indeed to have so excellent a memory."

Yeshu did not mean to rebuke him, but was only stating a moral fact when he replied, "Reverend Sir, I do not let myself have pride. I contemplate the glory of the Lord God of Israel." This was considered to be an excellent answer, and the murmur of admiration which went through the group of scholars may possibly have caused the desert boy some pride in spite of himself. But this could not have been for more than a moment. It was a wonderful occasion for him; he had an opportunity to learn, and all his faculties were concentrated upon doing so. He remembered the texts, he remembered the names of these learned gentlemen and every bit of the wisdom they imparted to him.

They could not invite him to eat with them, he being unclean. They bade Yehoiarib take him home and feed him, and then bring him into the Temple again for further talk. That afternoon they brought with them a distinguished scholar whom they all addressed with special respect, calling him *Nasi*, which means prince. Yeshu knew there had been princes in Israel but he had surely never expected to meet one. Later on he learned from his friend and guide that this gentleman had earned his title by being chosen head of the Sanhedrin, which was the council of the Jewish elders in Jerusalem. His name was Hillel, and he was one of the greatest of scholars, celebrated for his piety and humility, of which he made a cult.

He was one who would not turn aside from a desert child, or call him impure because he did not know the details of the ritual. He himself had come to Jerusalem as an emigrant from Babylonia—where many Jews had remained ever since the days of the captivity. He had come as a poor man, had worked with his hands as a smith, and had lived upon his wage of one-half a dinar—twelve and one-half cents a day. Now he had risen to be prince of the national council, but still he made a speciality of humility, greeting all men with love and kindness, and treating them all as sons of God. He even accepted proselytes, and treated them the same.

Yehoiarib had told a story about him—a funny story, for the Jews have a keen sense of humor, especially when it deals with their exalted ones. A certain man had made a wager of four hundred *zuz*, the equivalent of about a hundred dollars, the wager being that he could provoke Hillel to anger. He waited until the Sabbath eve, when Hillel would be occupied with preparations for the holy day, and then he stood outside his house and shouted for him. Hillel came, asking mildly, "What is it, my son?" The man proceeded to ask him a string

of the silliest questions he could think of. "Why are the
Babylonians long-headed?" and then, "Why are the eyes of
the Palmyreans red?" and "Why are the feet of the Africans
broad?" Each time Hillel answered mildly, and this, of course,
annoyed the man greatly because he had lost his wager. "Are
you," he exclaimed, "that Hillel whom they call the prince of
Israel? May there be few such among our people!" Hillel, surprised, inquired, "Why, my son?" and the answer was. "Because you have cost me four hundred *zuz!*"

Such was the kind gray-bearded gentleman who sat for an
hour or two and questioned little Yeshu of the desert, and gave
him advice and instruction. When he saw that the child really
was wise beyond his years, and eager to learn everything that
would help him in worship of and obedience to the God of
Israel, this scholar taught him some of his principles, and each
time Yeshu repeated his words and showed that he had not
merely learned them by heart but understood them. This
teacher of humility said, "My abatement is my exaltation"—
which might have been a hard saying to some of the wordly
ones who sat listening, but to Yeshu it was as the voice of his
own soul. And likewise when Hillel pronounced, "What is unpleasant to thyself, that do not do to thy neighbor; this is the
whole Law." Such was Yeshu's own idea of the Law, and it
did not have anything to do with the washing of olives, or
the preservation of the ashes of a red heifer. He heard it
gladly and stowed it away in his mind.

Again, Rabbi Hillel said, "Judge not thy neighbor until
thou art in his place." When he saw the eagerness of response
in the face of the boy, he knew that here was in the making a
man of moral fervor, a future teacher of righteousness. He
asked Yeshu if he would not like to stay in this Temple and
become a student of the Law. The boy, greatly surprised,
asked time to think it over, and the old gentleman said that
was wise.

16

The visitor spent a second night with his kind friend the gatekeeper, and they talked until late, as before. The Levite had
been immensely impressed by the attention which the scholars
had paid to this lad, and especially by the fact that he had
been honored with the attentions of the *Nasi* of the Sanhedrin.
A chance to become a student in the Temple and under such
high auspices was an opportunity of a lifetime; but Yeshu
explained that his father was not well and needed him.

Furthermore, he added, timidly, he himself was a child of the desert and truly afraid of the great city and its tumultuous life. He did not mention the most important reason, for fear of offending his host. In the desert he felt the presence of Adonai, the God of his fathers, but here in the city he felt only the presence of men, and so many of them greedy and noisy and forgetful of righteousness and love.

Nor did the conversation of Yehoiarib do much to change his mind. The Levite told of high life in Jerusalem and the ways of the rich. He told how the Romans had put up the office of the high priest to be sold, and the price which had been paid for it. He told of aristocratic priests who owned as much as a hundred vineyards and a hundred fields, and worked them with slaves. He told of the crimes that went on in the Roman palaces, the fornications, adulteries, even murders. He told the life story of Herod, called the Great, and it appeared that great men strode to power over the dead bodies of their rivals, and of even their relatives.

Herod, called the Great, had conquered Judea with a Roman army. He had killed forty-five members of the Sanhedrin who had opposed him, and had confiscated their properties. He had ordered wholesale slaughters by his troops. He had had a young high priest drowned, he had had two of his own sons strangled, and then had had his eldest son executed —and five days later he himself lay dead. What a career that was, and what a government for pious men to be living under! There had been a new king, one of Herod's sons, but he had been so incompetent that now the Romans had taken over the government, and the Jews had no longer any pretense of freedom; they had to obey a Roman consul whose only thought was the amount of taxes he could collect to please his Emperor Tiberius in Rome.

Such had been the tragic plight of the Israelites through most of their long history. Yehoiarib lamented: they had been conquered by Egyptians, by Assyrians, by Babylonians, Phoenecians, and Philistines, by Persians, Syrians, Macedonians, and Romans. It was the will of the Lord that this small people should live on a few thousand square miles of lands surrounded by immense empires which warred back and forth and trampled their fields. The Hebrew peoples had had to defend their Law, and the code of morals which Adonai had given them, against the sexuality of the Egyptians, the drunkenness of the Persians, the cruelty of the Romans, the idolatry of the worshipers of numerous false gods. The idle rich, the fashionables, were always running after novelties, and that meant foreign notions in worship. Again and again the one great God had raised up prophets to rebuke and shame the backsliders; but now it had been officially decreed by the Israelite council that the age of the prophets was at an end, and that the Lord would send no more. "It might be that the Lord will have something to say about that," thought little Yeshu.

17

Tired as he was, the desert boy went out into the courtyard and stood with his hands stretched up to his Heavenly Father in prayer. "Thy will be done," he prayed. Very certainly God's will was not being done in Jerusalem at present, and the lad tormented his soul trying to understand how such evil could be, why Adonai permitted it, and what He wished His children to do about it. Very certainly it was Adonai who had made these children, the Israelites, and chosen them for His own. Very certainly He could not wish them to go on living in sin; but how could they be changed, and who was to do it? It must be that He was moved to grief by what He witnessed. How long would it be before He was moved to wrath, and would send down His lightnings, or send in another enemy to destroy this so wicked city?

Then deep in his soul the lad felt that stirring which he had come to know as the indication of the presence of the Terrible One. Trembling seized him, joy filled his heart, and it was like a bright light shining within! He knew then that Adonai lived in Jerusalem as well as in the desert. He besought Adonai to give him some sign as to what he should do. Where would he find God and how would he learn to live with God?

Yeshu was young, he was weak, and he didn't even know his own soul very well. His prayers deepened his fear of this great city and of the people he had met in it. If he stayed with them, he might become like them; if he let them teach him, they would surely teach him to follow their example, and would hate him if he did not. To be sure Hillel the Prince was a good man, but he was one in a thousand; the Levite insisted upon that, and moreover Hillel was an old man and could not last long. If Yeshu stayed here he would learn to read, but he would have to spend his time reading the niceties of the Law and the disputations which the learned scribes had put into their Talmud and their Mishna and other holy commentaries. Was that what Yeshu really wanted?

The voice of Adonai in his soul answered No. These men worshiped the Law because of the fear they had in their souls, the fear to think for themselves. They had no consciousness of God in their hearts, they did not trust their hearts, they only could learn lessons by rote, make rules for themselves and others, and then try to follow them. When they disagreed about the rules, who was to say which was right? They had lost themselves in a wilderness of disputation. The letter killeth, the spirit giveth life!

Yeshu went to the Temple yet another day and listened to such of the learned men as wished to question him, and they marveled at his wisdom and the quickness of his mind; but he did not tell them his deepest thoughts. He did not tell his opinion of them, for that would not be polite, and he had never in his life thought of being impolite to one of his elders. But to the kind prince of the Sanhedrin he said that he had prayed over it and believed it was his duty to go back to his own people if he could find them. He would stay in the desert and put himself in the hands of his Heavenly Father, and stay there until this Heavenly Father sent him a definite command to re-enter the world. The kind prince agreed that this might be the wiser course.

18

Yeshu's family traveled a day's journey before they discovered that he was missing. When a women has six or more children, and is poor, she has to leave them to look after one another. Every one thought that Yeshu must be with other members of the large traveling group. When it was realized that he was missing Yosef and Marya left their children with the rest of the tribe, and appointed a meeting place at a well in the desert; then they went back to search for their lost lamb.

It was not easy to find him in that vast throng. They inquired everywhere but no one had seen him. When, after two days, they came upon him, they were surprised to find him seated in the Temple in the company of several learned doctors of the Law. The mother said, "Son, why hast thou thus dealt with us? behold thy father and I have sought thee sorrowing." And he said unto them, "How is it that ye sought me? wist ye not that I must be about my Father's business."

They did not understand that saying. They tried to think what business of Yosef he could have been talking about. It did not occur to them that it was Adonai the Lord of whom the child had spoken. Hillel had taught him the words of that wonderful last song which Moses had sung to "all the congregation of Israel" just before he went up to Mount Nebo to die. He had called them a perverse and crooked generation —this more than fourteen centuries before Yeshu's time. He had "published the name of the Lord." and commanded: "Ascribe ye greatness unto our God. He is the Rock, His work is perfect: for all his ways are judgment: a God of truth and without iniquity, just and right is He." And then Moses had reminded them that God was their Father. "Is not He thy Father that hath bought thee? Hath He not made thee, and established thee?" So Yeshu had taken up this strange way of speaking, beyond the comprehension of his earthly parents. He had outgrown them mentally, and they were in awe of him, but at the same time worried because his ways were not like those of his brothers.

On the way he told them where he had stayed, the people he had met, what he had had to eat. But he did not try to tell them about the conversations, or the new thoughts which had been started in his mind. He knew that the opinions he had formed of Jerusalem would be beyond the scope of their understanding and would frighten them. From now on his thoughts would be between himself and his Heavenly Father, who understood everything, even without any word being spoken. This is a secret life which every man carries in his own heart.

Back into the desert, which was the Lord's place. It was quiet there. The sun rose in majesty, revealing the power of the Lord, also His wrath, because it was a terrible thing in the heat of the day. All the desert creatures hid from it. But when it had sunk low in the sky, then the creatures came forth and scurried here and there. The Lord had been merciful to them, making them of colors so that they were not easy to find; but even so, the serpents knew them and slid stealthily along the ground in pursuit. The birds were few, and lean; they had long legs with which they ran quickly; they did not fly unless they were forced to. Heat and drought ruled all their lives.

When darkness had come, and the stars shone, then was the time for a lad to steal out into the solitude and lift his hands in prayer. The shimmering lights above were like those in his own soul, and in the peace and stillness he could hear the inner voice, speaking to him and telling him that the world which God had created was a wonderful place, and it was only the sins of men which made it evil. God had set the stars "in the firmament of the heaven to give light upon the earth, and to rule over the day and the night, and to divide the light from the dark: and God saw that it was good."

Everything everywhere was of God; all power was His. As Yeshu's mind unfolded and he was able to understand problems which had puzzled him, this process was God's revelation, this was His gift, opening like flowers in his soul. Every day he recited psalms, giving thanks for the light which had come, and praying for more light and seeing that come. He went apart and prayed more frequently than ever, for now he knew how great was the need of the Hebrew people for the help of their God. He questioned his own tribe, and those he met at the desert wells, and those who traveled and stopped with them. He learned much about what was going on in the land, and about the strange new ideas and sects which existed; but he himself clung closely to the ancient prophets. His mind grew and his discourse acquired authority. Men marveled at him.

He had brought with him out of Jerusalem a small piece of parchment which had been given him by Yehoiarib; it was priceless because the Levite had written on it all the letters of the Hebrew alphabet. The lad studied them diligently. He could not remember all the sounds which these letters stood for, but in course of time he made inquiry of travelers, and so picked up the rest of the information. Then it was wonderful, because by putting these sounds together he could shape a word and see how it looked. Knowing so many psalms and prayers as he did, he entertained himself by figuring out how they would look when written. It would have been a wrong thing to draw pictures in the desert sand, but there was no harm in marking words, for they were words of God. He had given them to Moses on tablets.

This was an exciting adventure, a game for one who had never played any sort of game hitherto. It made Yeshu still more wonderful to his tribesmen, who had never before seen anyone learning either to read or write. In the schools, where as children they had sometimes sat in the villages, reading and writing were for the poor an unthought-of art; the lessons consisted of the reciting of holy texts. But Yeshu kept at his game consistently, checking his guesses every time he encountered anyone who possessed knowledge of the two great secrets.

19

After a year or two, Yeshu's father died. In that hot climate it was necessary that a body should be buried quickly,
so they took him into the desert. Because the ground was hard
and stony, they were not able to dig deep, therefore they
piled heavy stones, making a sort of monument. It was necessary that the body should not be touched by wild beasts,
because in the time to come it would be resurrected and
restored; and Yeshu had become certain that this time would
be soon. After he had done his share of this labor, he was
tired, but he did not feel unclean, in spite of all that the
scribes and Pharisees had attempted to teach him.

Under Jewish custom Yeshu's mother now became the wife
of her deceased husband's older brother. This man lived in the
outskirts of the town of Nazareth, where by marriage he had
acquired a small property. So the Rechabite tribe escorted
the widow and her four sons and two daughters to this place.
Baaseiah was the man's name, and he was good and pious,
and knew that it was his duty to take in this family; more
important yet his first wife knew that it was her duty under
God to be kind to the second wife.

The home had only two small rooms, so the four boys had
to help build a sort of shed attached to the stable where the
animals lived. There they slept and were well pleased, because they loved the animals, and it was more comfort than
they had known in the desert wanderings. Baaseiah was a
potter, and had his workshed on the place. He taught this
trade to Yeshu's brother, Ya'akob—a name which has become
two different names in English, Jacob and James. Yeshu
had learned carpentry from his father, and could make very
good well pulleys, also plow yokes; but it was hard work
and exhausting, and when he had put in a full day he was
almost too tired to stand up and pray. He was well pleased
when Baaseiah proposed that he should take care of the
animals.

The stepfather-uncle owned a flock of half a dozen sheep
and goats, and it became Yeshu's duty to lead them out into
the hills and watch over them while they grazed. There were
no fences, so the smallest flock had to have a shepherd. This
duty gave pleasure to a growing lad, for he loved to look at
the beautiful land of Galilee, which was one great garden,
with vineyards and olive groves climbing the slopes of the
hills.

To Yeshu the creatures were a special gift from the Lord. From them came milk, wool for clothing, every year a lamb for the sacrifice, and others to be sold for taxes to the Romans. Watching them, he could observe the wonders of the world which God had made; he could meditate upon these and recite to himself the thanksgiving psalms of the prophets. When people saw him standing far out upon the lonely hills in an attitude of prayer they were reminded of their own religious duties, and resolved to perform them—but generally put it off till the next day.

20

The town of Nazareth consisted of perhaps two hundred mud-walled houses scattered pretty much haphazard. It was a market town, and the peasants brought in their produce, and there were shops which exhibited goods of various kinds. To a desert lad these were interesting sights; he had no money to buy anything, but he had no needs, and therefore no sense of deprivation. Most of all he liked the town because it had a synagogue. This was an institution which had come into being in the days of the captivity in Babylon. Before that the Jews had been permitted to have only the one Temple; but in Babylon, having no Temple, they had set up little meeting places where they could gather and hear the Law read and the scriptures recited. When they had come back from Babylon they had brought this institution with them.

So in Nazareth was this one-roomed structure where the people gathered on the Sabbath. It was made of bricks, baked in the sun, each brick two feet square and about three inches high, so that the walls were solid and withstood the weather. Timbers had been cut for the roof and for the benches inside, and there was a learned man who combined the functions of janitor and priest. His name was Mahalaleel, which means praise of God. He had a long gray beard, a pious soul, and a kindly disposition. He had been a student scribe of the Temple in Jerusalem, but had left it because of discontent with the treatment he received there. In Nazareth he had what he considered an ideal life. He worked as a wheelwright, and in spare time took care of the altar and the seven-branched candle-stick, and of the capsa in which a dozen sacred scrolls were preserved. Alongside the synagogue he had a one-room hut in which his elderly wife kept their home. God had blessed them with long life, and both were tireless in thanksgiving.

48   THE SECRET LIFE OF JESUS

It did not take long for Yeshu to become acquainted with
this man, nor did it take the man long to realize that here was
a prematurely old mind in a young body. In the course of time
Yeshu learned everything that Mahalaleel knew. That included not merely to read and write slowly and carefully, but
the recital of many Hebrew prayers and psalms, and the
meaning of their words; it included a mass of traditions from
the Talmud and the Talmud Babli, from the Mishna, the
Tosefta, and the Midrashim. There were proverbs, sayings,
stories, and commentaries on the way of life of pious Jews.

Mahalaleel was a man of Galilee. He had gone to Jerusalem,
like Yeshu, full of enthusiasm for the Holy City and its Temple; but as the years passed he had become embittered against
the men of Judah, who now ruled and ran the Temple, and
used it for their own enrichment and glory. They looked upon
Galileans as social inferiors, and treated them harshly. So
Mahalaleel had come back to the scenes of his childhood, and
now he labored to impress upon his pupil a distrust of the
priests and Pharisees. The priests had made their terms with
the idolatrous Romans; a few had acquired wealth, and lived
luxurious lives, and had appropriated to themselves all the
glory of Israel. It was a crime, for glory belonged to the
Lord, and he had intended it for all His chosen people, and
not merely for one tribe, that of Judah.

Yeshu, being a son of David, was of the tribe himself; but
living in Galilee and knowing the people, his sympathies were
divided. With all his heart he desired that there should be no
strife among the members of the house of Israel. He wanted
all men to live at peace and do justice to one another. For him
the Law was summed up in one verse from the book of Leviticus, "Thou shalt not avenge, or bear any grudge against
the children of thy people; thou shalt love thy neighbor as
thyself: I am the Lord." To Yeshu that was a command from
the Maker and Master of all the earth, and of all the people
who lived upon it. He could not understand why men did not
obey this clear and simple instruction. Daily he went into the
lonely places, raised his hands to his Heavenly Father, and
implored Him to tell His humble son the reason for the
wickedness in the hearts of men.

So the prophets of Israel had been doing for a thousand
years, and the history and literature of that people were full
of their lamentations, exhortations, and threats of doom.
Mahalaleel had stored his mind with the utterances of these
men; that was what his years of study had been for, and

nothing could make him happier than to teach the words to an eager lad who seldom had to hear them repeated. They were recited as a chant, in a mood of exaltation. Not merely did Mahalaleel know the words of the great poets, he also knew something about their biographies, and would tell Yeshu stories which brought the living men before his young eyes, and explained the mysteries which lurked in the ancient texts.

21

First among these messengers of God stood the magnificent Isaiah. He had been a rich man and an aristocrat, brought up in Jerusalem amid all its wickedness. The Hebrew people had then been living under the overlordship of the Assyrians, who were warring with the Babylonians and also the Egyptians; so it had been a hard time for a pacifist. But the Lord commanded Isaiah to keep his people out of this war and save his holy city from destruction. Also the Lord bade him speak out against the injustices which all men could see in the city, the oppressions of the poor by the rich. In magnificent exhortations a great prophet spoke, and the young son of the desert learned the holy words; when he sat on the hillside tending his little flock, he recited them both to himself and to the Lord above who heard him.

Isaiah had repudiated sacrifices, and all that ritual of blood and commercialism which had so disturbed Yeshu in Jerusalem. "Hear the word of the Lord, ye rulers of Sodom; give ear unto the law of our God, ye people of Gomorrah. To what purpose is the multitude of your sacrifices unto Me? saith the Lord: I am full of the burnt offerings of rams, and the fat of fed beasts; and I delight not in the blood of bullocks, or of lambs, or of the goats. When ye come to appear before Me, who hath required this at your hand, to tread My courts? Bring no more vain oblations; incense is an abomination unto Me; the new moons and sabbaths, the calling of assemblies, I cannot away with; it is iniquity, even the solemn meeting. Your new moons and your appointed feasts My soul hateth: they are a trouble unto Me; I am weary to bear them. And when ye spread forth your hands, I will hide Mine eyes from you: yea, when ye make many prayers, I will not hear: your hands are full of blood. Wash you, make you clean; put away the evil of your doings from before Mine eyes; cease to do evil; learn to do well; seek judgment, relieve the oppressed, judge the fatherless, plead for the widow. Come now, and let us reason together, saith the Lord: though your sins be as

scarlet, they shall be as white as snow; though they be red
like crimson, they shall be as wool. If ye be willing and obedient, ye shall eat the good of the land: But if ye refuse and
rebel, ye shall be devoured with the sword: for the mouth of
the Lord hath spoken it."

There were people of relative wealth, even in the small town
of Nazareth; people who owned land and slaves, and could put
their burdens off on others. Here, too, the poor were oppressed, widows were deprived of their homes, and orphans
had to work long hours without sufficient food, as had often
been the case with Yeshu himself. So the lad was shaken to the
deeps of his soul by the holy man's words: "The Spirit of the
Lord God is upon me; because the Lord hath anointed me to
preach good tidings unto the meek; He hath sent me to bind
up the brokenhearted, to proclaim liberty to the captives, and
the opening of the prison to them that are bound; to proclaim the acceptable year of the Lord, and the day of vengeance of our God; to comfort all that mourn; to anoint unto
them that mourn in Zion, to give unto them beauty for ashes,
the oil of joy for mourning, the garment of praise for the
spirit of heaviness; that they might be called trees of righteousness, the planting of the Lord, that He might be glorified."

22

Every word of these ancient men was sacred to Yeshu; he
was sure that every word had been directly dictated by the
Almighty. The things which Mahalaleel told him made them
as teachers and friends to him; they walked and talked with
him, and their words fitted to a similar time of wickedness, of
treason to the Most High. There was the angry Jeremiah, a
countryman who had come up to Jerusalem, and like
Mahalaleel and like Yeshu had been shocked by what he had
seen. How he did scold the rich and haughty ones, with no
sparing of their feelings!

"For among my people are found wicked men: they lay
wait, as he that setteth snares; they set a trap, they catch
men. As a cage is full of birds, so are their houses full of
deceit: therefore they are become great, and waxen rich. They
are waxen fat, they shine: yea, they overpass the deeds of the
wicked: they judge not the cause, the cause of the fatherless,
yet they prosper; and the right of the needy do they not
judge. Shall I not visit for these things? said the Lord: shall
not My soul be avenged on such a nation as this? A wonderful

and horrible thing is committed in the land; the prophets
prophesy falsely, and the priests bear rule by their means;
and my people love to have it so: and what will ye do in the
end thereof?"

This had been just before the coming of the Babylonians,
and Jeremiah had lived to see his terrible prophecies come
true. He had seen Jerusalem captured and destroyed. He had
been taken to Babylon among the exiles, and later had been
carried off a captive to Egypt; but nowhere had he failed to
raise his voice in command to the Hebrews to remember their
own Adonai, the true God, and to have nothing to do with the
false gods of their conquerors. Yeshu wondered, could it be his
fortune to live and see the city of the Lord destroyed at the
Lord's command?

Still closer to Yeshu's soul was the prophet Amos, who had
come from Tekoa, south of Jerusalem, a stony land which
barely yielded a living to its people. He had earned his bread
by dressing sycamore trees, and later by tending sheep and
oxen. There was nothing he did not know about country life,
and when he came to town and saw the ways of the rich, he
owed them no respect, nor even politeness. He spoke not for
himself, but for the Most High. "I hate, I despise your feast
days, and I will not smell in your solemn assemblies. Though
ye offer me burnt offerings and your meat offerings, I will not
accept them: neither will I regard the peace offerings of your
fat beasts. Take thou away from me the noise of thy songs;
for I will not hear the melody of thy viols. But let judgment
run down as waters, and righteousness as a mighty stream."
Learning such words, and pondering them, Yeshu became a
young "radical," questioning authority, and at war with the
powers that ruled his time.

23

Also there was Ezekiel, a man from the north country, the
fiercest of all. He, too, was of peasant origin, and employed
the crude language of peasants, shocking to refined ears, even
in the days of little Yeshu. He pictured two sisters, one of
them Samaria and the other Jerusalem. These sisters had gone
a-whoring, and what they had done in the course of their evil
life was so terrible that a sensitive lad could hardly bear to
hear about it.

The Babylonian captivity had come, and Ezekiel had been
carried away. He had to earn his living as a craftsman,
and so he had come to sympathize with the poor and to under-

stand their feelings. A man familiar with the life of shepherds, he had rebuked the false shepherds who neglected their flocks. "The word of the Lord came unto me, saying, Son of man, prophesy against the shepherds of Israel, prophesy and say unto them, Thus saith the Lord God unto the shepherds: Woe be to the shepherds of Israel that do feed themselves! Should not the shepherds feed the flocks? Ye eat the fat, and ye clothe you with the wool, ye kill them that are fed: but ye feed not the flock. Ye My flock, the flock of My pasture, are men, and I am your God, saith the Lord God."

A tragic life this old prophet had lived, for he had seen his people worshiping the Babylonian gods and setting up idols in a new temple they had built. He had had to invent secret symbols in order to rebuke them; every Israelite understood what these symbols meant, but the Babylonians had not understood. Ezekiel had invented a name for himself as prophet, the Son of Man, and this phrase fascinated Yeshu. He prayed to the Lord to send a new Son of Man who would rebuke the wickedness of this time. Also, he learned from Ezekiel the device of speaking in parables. The Romans were as cruel as the Babylonians, but also as stupid, and would not understand meanings which every Hebrew would instantly get. "Be ye wise as the serpent and as gentle as the dove," said Mahalaleel, and Yeshu made note of the advice.

In the spirit of these mighty poets, Yeshu prayed daily for spiritual help. He laid siege to Adonai—a favorite practice of the Hebrews. The Lord God was just, the Lord God was righteous, and knew a just and righteous man when He saw one. He heard the prayers that were ascending to Him and judged them. He was a stern Father, but also just, and could be indulgent. He could be moved and forced to action; He could even be troubled, and made to do something about the evils which a petitioner kept impressing upon His mind. "The sacrifice of the wicked is an abomination to the Lord: but the prayer of the upright is His delight: the way of the wicked is an abomination unto the Lord: but He loveth him who followeth after righteousness. . . . Hell and destruction are before the Lord: how much more than are the children of men."

The God of Israel was a jealous God, He had said that Himself; He could also be an angry God; He was Shaddai, The Terrible One. But also He was a loving God, and had commanded all his children to love Him, and to love one another. "Have we not all one Father?" the prophet Malachi had cried. "Hath not one God created us?" These words were taught to Yeshu when he was a child, and he never forgot them; they became the guiding theme of his life. He took them quite literally, and he walked and thought and lived with his Heavenly Father all the rest of his days on earth. He wanted other men to do the same, and strove with all his heart to teach them and guide them in accordance with that idea.

It could hardly have occurred to him that the Lord might intend him to become a prophet. He was young, and never dreamed of putting himself forward. What he prayed was, that the Lord would send a new prophet to be Yeshu's master and guide. He wanted to see righteousness come back to Israel, but he could not see how it might happen. The great and good Hillel had died, and there was no one like him. Yeshu remembered the Pharisees and the Sadducees who had mocked, and whose business it was to reduce religion to ritual. If any prophet came to them, speaking the things which the prophets of old had spoken, they would surely stone him.

Also there seemed to be nothing that could be done in the world of government or of business affairs. Here the Romans ruled, and ruled sternly. Justice to them meant obedience to Roman law; love meant nothing that Yeshu could ever see any sign of in their behavior. He had seen the Roman soldiers walking in the street, and had made note how the Hebrews kept out of their way. Any Roman soldier had the right to command any conquered man to carry his burden as far as the soldier wished; so if a Hebrew saw one coming on the highway, he went off it quickly. Every Roman soldier carried a short double-bladed sword, sharp and deadly. He seldom had to draw it; if he laid his hand upon it that was enough. Every Jew knew how many thousands had been slain, and how many would be slain if there was any sort of tumult or protest. If a man were to arise and proclaim defiance to the Roman law, they had a cruel form of execution. They would nail two pieces of wood together, forming a cross, and would nail the man's wrists to that cross and then set it up in the ground, braced with stones, and there he would hang for a day, two days, or three, until he was dead. Then his relatives might take him down and bury him; the Romans would not trouble themselves with that.

24

Yeshu helped his stepfather, and helped his mother, and his younger brothers and sisters. He grew in body as well as in mind, and presently came those changes which told him that he was becoming a man. This brought new problems, as it does to every man. It might be thought that Yeshu with his physical frailty would not be attractive to women, but this was far from the case. He had lovely dark eyes, a sweet and gentle face, and his words were like magic to them. Some trusted him, and would have loved him; but what could a poor lad do about marriage? In this heavily-taxed country an artisan would have to work until his middle years in order to save up enough to purchase a wife, and after that to take care of a family. Under the Jewish custom, no proper father would let his daughter go without a price; he would feel disgraced if he did not exact it—though frequently, when times were hard, it was the custom to accept a token price.

Yeshu, a youth who heard a call in his soul, could make no plans of that sort, and neither could he go a-whoring after the fashion of others in this time of moral decay. All the prophets whom he loved and honored railed against fornication, and still more against adultery. Yeshu was sure that Adonai would never listen to the voice of one who had polluted himself. For a man who wished to enter the service of the Lord, even informally, there was only one course possible; he must become an ascetic like the Essenes, a sect of the time about whose devout practices Yeshu had heard. To do that was not easy; but when he felt temptation stirring within him, he knew that it was Satan, the antagonist, at work, and he hastened apart and raised his hands in prayer. He asked the Lord to help him, and the Lord always did so.

There is another recourse, likewise known to holy men; that is fasting. When you abstain from food your body becomes weak and your sexual power also. Under the guidance of Mahalaleel, Yeshu learned to fast, and this proved to be an excellent thing from the point of view of a poor man. He could not do hard work, but he could go out and tend the sheep and goats, and his stepfather-uncle was well content not to have to provide him with food. Fasting was a most honorable thing among the Hebrews, and Yeshu was looked upon with awe by both men and women. They realized that they had a wonder child among them, and would ask him timidly whether God had spoken to him up in the hills, and what He had said. They were just as sure as Yeshu was that the Lord was up there, and while they frequently broke His laws and sinned, they always did so with fear and trembling, and were prepared to have some penalty fall upon their heads.

25

Nazareth was a poor town and had never had any sort of distinction. Yeshu had been born there, so his mother told him. One time the Rechabite tribe had been traveling, and as the inn was crowded they had sought shelter for the night in a stable. Then Marya's time had come, and the child had been a boy, and she had rejoiced as a Hebrew woman always did. They had wrapped the babe in a cloth and laid it in the manger; and now Marya pointed out that manger to Yeshu. The information did not surprise or trouble him, for to him a stable was a pleasant place, with the warm smell of animals; a manger was as clean and proper a place for a babe as any that he knew.

Animals were a part of everyday life to him; they followed him and he followed them; they sustained his life, and he sustained theirs. His language was full of references to them; and the same thing was true of the charming landscape of Galilee, the hills, the valleys, the fig trees, the vineyards, the harvests and the threshing floors. It was a countryman's life that he now lived, and a countryman's God he worshiped. The fact that he did carpentry work made no difference, for he did it for other country people like himself. He had been only once to a large city, and told himself that he would never go again.

26

The youth grew and increased in wisdom, and in favor with God and man. Whatever he was doing with his hands his inner life never changed. It was a search for God and for peace on earth. His prayers were an incessant plea to God to redeem the world, and to save it from the cruelties and crimes that were going on in the great cities.

God himself must come to redeem His world; or at the least He must send a Messiah. The ancient prophets appeared to differ in their ideas as to whether this Anointed One would be a heavenly being sent down by God, or whether he would be some man raised up to do God's work. Of late the hope had been abandoned by a beaten people. Malachi had been the last of the prophets, nearly five hundred years ago, and the people had become discouraged and had weakened in their faith.

Yeshu longed to know what the old teachings had been, and he besought his friend Mahalaleel to give him the exact words.

This, alas, was rarely possible, since the Levite had only a few scrolls, and for the rest relied upon his memory. The prophecy in Isaiah seemed clear enough, and it indicated that it was going to be a human Messiah. "For unto us a child is born, unto us a son is given: and the government shall be upon his shoulder: and his name shall be called Wonderful, Counsellor, The mighty God, The everlasting Father, The Prince of Peace. Of the increase of his government and peace there shall be no end, upon the throne of David, and upon his kingdom, to order it, and to establish it with judgment and with justice from henceforth even for ever. The zeal of the Lord of hosts will perform this."

On the other hand a prophecy in Daniel was confusing, and it was difficult to know what to make of it. Here was a promise of the Messiah, the Prince, whose coming would be only seven weeks "from the going forth of the commandment to restore and to build Jerusalem." It went on to specify numbers of weeks for other events, and it was hard to make out what the time referred to might be. Yeshu couldn't make head or tail of it, and worried his patient old friend. How could the Lord have left the matter so obscure?

Finally the friend invited him for a walk, and after solemnly pledging him to silence, imparted a grave secret. He, who had dwelt in the Temple, and had studied to become a scribe, had known many of the learned ones, and had listened to the whispers that went about. One must not place too much faith in the written words, or let one's mind be confused by contradictions in the texts, for all the old scrolls were far from reliable. They were supposed to be the directly dictated or inspired words of God, but how often had presumptuous men sought to impose their ideas upon mankind in God's name!

Take the old book called Genesis. It was supposed to go back to the creation of the world, four thousand years ago, and to the time of Abraham, two thousand years ago; but was there any record as old as that? Had anyone ever seen a scroll that went back to those days? Surely there were no such scrolls in Jerusalem, which had been burnt and razed by the Babylonians six hundred years ago.

Mahalaleel revealed to Yeshu that the priests and the scribes in the days of the return to Jerusalem had set themselves to saving the Israelites from further contamination by the dreadful gods whom they had been forced publicly to worship in Babylon, and whom, in their hearts, they had cursed. From now on God's chosen people must become the strictest monotheists, and their ancient books must be rewritten to impress that doctrine upon them. Their history must be made to show them as having been monotheists at all times. The utterances of Yahweh must be caused to preach that doctrine, and their stories must inspire gratitude to the Almighty One who had guarded and guided them through the centuries. So it had been done with the history in *Genesis* and *Exodus*, and with the teachings and laws in *Leviticus, Numbers,* and *Deuteronomy.*

Stranger yet, and more shocking to the soul of a pious youth, passages had been inserted in order to take the glory away from the people of Galilee and give it to the people of Judea. It was the latter who had come back from the exile, and were setting out to rebuild Jerusalem, and they must be shown as having had the support of the Most High, and having been through the ages His chosen agents. Most of the Benjaminites and Ephraimites had been carried off by the Assyrians and had never been allowed to come back; so now for five centuries the glory had shone upon the tribe of Judah, which in the earliest days had hardly been considered Israelite at all. They had made themselves the center of history, so that now the people of all Israel were called Jews instead of Israelites. Yeshu was a Jew; but Mahalaleel didn't want to be! He wanted to be of his own tribe.

27

The Israelite history had started with Father Abram, a herdsman of the wild country. The Lord had told him to get out of that country into a new land which the Lord would show him. "And I will make of thee a great nation, and I will bless thee and make thy name great, and thou shalt be a blessing." Abram was seventy-five years old when he departed out of the land of Haran. He settled in the land of Canaan, and had many adventures, including a trip to Egypt; occasionally the Lord came and sat down by him in the heat of the day, and gave him instructions about how to build altars and about the future of the Hebrew race. The Lord told him that he would change his name to Abraham, which means father of a great multitude; and he was surely that. He lived to be a hundred and eighty-five; he had several wives, and to his son Isaac the Lord appeared and said, "I will make thy seed to multiply as the stars of Heaven, and will give unto thy seed all these countries; and in thy seed shall all the nations of the earth be blessed."

Jacob, the second son of Isaac, got his old father's blessing by pretending to be his older brother Esau. Then he went away and worked for seven years to win one of two sisters whom he loved, but their father gave him the wrong one, a scurvy trick. Jacob worked for seven years more and earned the other sister, and so he had two wives, and they didn't get along very well together. To modern eyes the story of these two ladies and their husband, not to mention two extra hand-maidens, and the various quarrels they had among themselves and their many children—all this might seem somewhat comical. But it surely did not seem so to Yeshu, because this was the beginning of the founding of his people, and to his mind every word of it had been holy up to that time. God had told them to be fruitful, multiply, and replenish the earth.

But now it was revealed that many of these words were not the words of God at all; the story of the barrenness of Rachel, and how she had had children born by her handmaiden instead of herself, and how later the Lord remedied her barrenness and gave her children—all these details had been inserted by priests a thousand years later, in order to give glory to the tribe of Judah. God had been shown granting fertility to Leah, who had become the mother of Reuben, Simeon, and Levi, Judah, Issachar, and Zebulun—these being the six tribes whom the priests of the Jews wished to favor and put forward. Mahalaleel said that the text was full of contradictions, so that you could know it was not the true word of God. He was sure, because he had been permitted to take the sacred scrolls out of the capsa and look up the phrases for himself.

Yeshu, child of the desert, had had an image of some holy man sitting with a roll of parchment before him, and listening while the Lord dictated the text word by word in the ancient Hebrew language. Not even the priests knew it now; many of them recited prayers and psalms without knowing what any of the words meant. Many were so ignorant that they couldn't even read the Aramaic language they spoke. From Mahalaleel he now learned that holy books were copied by humble scribes, many of them slaves, who sat in a room, each with a roll of parchment before him, while a single man, the dictator, read aloud from the text, and every scribe copied what he heard. If a dictator came to a passage which he did not like, he could leave it out, or change it, and all the copyists would copy what they heard and be none the wiser. It might be that some priest or doctor of the law would take it upon himself to decide that something should be revised; or he might claim that the Lord had spoken to him in a dream—anyhow, he would mark out some passage and write something else in the margin, and the new manuscripts would be copied that way.

Among other things the elderly teacher convinced Yeshu that he would have to give up his wonder dream of the holy Tabernacle which had been set up for two million wandering people. It was all a phantasy; nothing like it had ever existed in reality. When you stopped to think you could realize that it was rather absurd to imagine twenty-two thousand men carrying a building through the desert all over southern Arabia— over a period of forty years. The story had been invented in order to teach piety to the Jewish people; the priests had described the imaginary Tabernacle as corresponding in all ways to the actual Temple they were rebuilding in Jerusalem. They quoted the Lord as giving the most choice camp site to the tribe of Judah, in front of the Tabernacle, facing the rissing sun. That would inspire the Israelites with more respect for Judah, and help to turn them all into Jews!

So said the elderly man of Galilee, who had quarreled with his masters and hated the ignorant priests who had dominated him. The Pharisees and Sadducees, his teachers, had affronted him with their arrogance, and even had beaten him on half-a-dozen occasions because of his mistakes. He, a humble poor man from Galilee, one of the 'am ha-aretz, was the scum of the Israelite earth.

From all this Yeshu learned that the world was an even worse place than he had imagined it. It did not even respect the sacred words which, at some time, Yahweh must have dictated to His people. A man who wished to worship God in spirit and in truth had to realize how the letter killeth, while only the spirit giveth life. Yeshu came more and more to distrust the learned ones, who made it their pride to interpret texts, and would spend whole days wrangling over the precise meaning of a phrase. He learned to distrust the priesthood which was seeking worldly power and applause, and spent its time going through elaborate ceremonies while forgetting justice and the love of God.

From that time the Rechabite *harash* was a rebel, not merely against idol worship, but against the corrupted system of Jewish law and tradition. Religious life consisted of the disputes of two rival sects of priests and scribes, one the Pharisees and the other the Sadducees, which in reality were political parties striving for office, power, and wealth. The criterion of success was the ability, not merely to recite and interpret the subtleties and complications of ancient texts, but to pull wires and browbeat others, and win the favor of Roman masters by intrigues and bribes.

28

When Yeshu's younger brothers and sisters were grown up and able to take care of themselves, he was a free man, and he traveled to see the world. By now he was a skilled carpenter; a small man, but active and enduring. He would do enough work to pay for his food and lodging, and then he would sit and engage his employers in conversation—always, of course, on one subject, God and His dealings with the Israelite peoples.

The population of Galilee was half gentile, and all the foreign peoples had their gods; there were altars to a local Baal in the smaller villages. Also among the Hebrews many strange notions had taken root. There was the Sect of Damascus; there were New Covenanters, who, like Jesus, opposed the priesthood; there were Water Drinkers, Morning Bathers, Worshipers at Sunrise—a score of such groups, and you never knew what you would find in the next house. In the old days an angel had been a messenger from the Lord, and he had been an impersonal being; but by now the Pharisees had invented a great number of angels with names, and had all sorts of legends to tell about them. Satan had been brought in by the prophet Zechariah, and was supposed to be an evil being; but by now there were a variety of satans and you could take your choice among them.

The Hebrews were lacking in the gift for abstract thought which the Greeks had cultivated so diligently. The Hebrews were hardly aware of themselves, and did not speculate about their minds; everything with them was ordered by God, everything was explained by this concept. The Lord was thanked for all benefits and blamed for all evils—even for the sinfulness of Israel. Cried the prophet Ezekiel, "Why dost Thou cause us to err from Thy ways, and harden our hearts that we fear Thee not?" Against this attitude it was difficult for a moralist like Yeshu to make progress. What good did it do to urge people to behave themselves, when they were convinced that it was God who caused them to misbehave?

There was a brotherhood scattered throughout Judea and Galilee called the Essenes. They had existed for a century or two, and we do not know what their name came from. They were strictly communistic in their way of life, owning no private property. They were ascetics, celibates and vegetarians, repudiating animal sacrifices, slavery and war. They practised the ancient Jewish rite of baptism, the washing away of sins by water. They had secret doctrines which were taught only to their initiates. They hoped by ascetic practices and prayers to come into possession of prophetic powers, and to be able to work miracles. They lived on little farms, rose before sunrise, prayed together, and worked until noon. Then they washed and put on white garments and sat down to a sacramental meal. After their meal they resumed their common dress and labor until evening, when again they ate together. They observed the Sabbath scrupulously, and received their education in classes. They were strict predestinarians, and believed in the transmigration of souls.

In many ways these were people after Yeshu's heart. He visited and lived among them for a time, but he never joined them. For one thing, he was no predestinarian; he believed in the freedom of the individual to choose right or wrong, and to change and renew his spirit. Also he believed in marriage. Most important of all, he did not believe in secrecy, in any sort of esoteric doctrine. God was in our hearts, He was in the heart of every man, He would speak to every man who prayed to Him. No intermediary, no priest was needed, no magician, no wonder worker. The Lord is a living God, and He lives in us and we in Him. His message is the love in our heart and not the words in holy books.

All this was no discovery of Yeshu; it was found in all the prophets, it was found even back in Deuteronomy, stated so explicitly that it was as if the Lord Himself had been trying to lay it down and make it impossible for the dullest mind in the world ever to misunderstand it. "For this commandment which I command thee this day, it is not hidden from thee, neither is it far off. It is not in heaven, that thou shouldest say, Who shall go up for us to heaven, and bring it unto us, that we may hear it, and do it? Neither is it beyond the sea, that thou shouldest say, Who shall go over the sea for us, and bring it unto us, that we may hear it, and do it? But the word is very nigh unto thee, in thy mouth, and in thy heart, that thou mayest do it." (DEUTERONOMY 30:11–14)

29

The tribe of the Rechabites came into Galilee, the relatives
and old friends of Yeshu whom he loved; he wandered again
with them and shared their vicissitudes. They were the real
people, the simple people, the footloose ones; the Hebrews had
a name for them, which was *barjonim*, meaning the outsiders,
or people of the outside, of the wide open spaces. They had
not fallen victim to the disease of civilization, they had not
acquired possessions and obligations, they were free to leave
everything and serve the Lord; so they did. Yeshu was a man
now, their man, their kind of man; when he went out and
stood in the desert to pray, they found nothing strange about
it, whether it was by day or night. They respected him because he was a man of God and acted on his faith. He was
wiser than they and set apart. There was something wonderful
about him, something great, and they knew it.

When he worked with them, he told them the things he had
learned, and they listened gladly. When the work was done
and they sat by the campfire, he talked about what God had
done for their forefathers, and how He was now present at
this moment listening to them, aware of what they were saying, doing, thinking and planning. All this was the stuff of
which their minds were made, their traditions and the lives of
their people for centuries and millennia in the past. This was
their faith, their hope, the very Presence of the living God.
Yeshu traveled with them back into the desert, and on the way,
in the quietness of the night when they were sure that no hostile ears were listening, that no spies of either the Romans or
the Pharisees were near, they told him of visits they had had
from the wild men, the real *barjonim*, the outlaws and rebels
against the existing empire.

Never, never would resistance die out among the Hebrews:
resistance to imperial Rome, the land of false gods and slavery, and likewise to those traitors to the Hebrew race, the
rich and educated of the cities who had made peace with the
Romans, with the abomination of desolation. As far back as
the childhood of Yosef, Yeshu's father, there had been a fierce
uprising of the Galileans against Herod who had obtained the
throne through the Roman power. It had been headed by a
zealot named Hizqiah, and it had been put down with terrible
slaughter. Again, some forty years later, when it became
known that Herod was on his death-bed, there had been more
uprising under the leadership of the son of Hizqiah, known

as Judas of Galilee. The Zealots had destroyed the golden
eagle at the gate of the Temple, and again there had been
bloody repression—but they did not care, because they were
firm in the conviction that if they sacrificed their lives in the
service of the Divine One they would attain immortality.

Then again, immediately after Herod died, there had been
another uprising. The people had crowded into the sanctuary
and demanded of Archelaus, the son of Herod and heir to the
throne, that he place a pure high priest in the place of the
favorite who had been chosen by Herod, and who was a wor-
shiper of Greek culture and likewise of Greek idols. There had
been terrible slaughter, some thirty thousand people had
entered into immortal glory, and the rebel leaders had re-
treated, as usual to the mountains and the deserts.

This time they had chosen as their leader a Rechabite, one
of those sons of David whose name was Yohanan ben Zekharya, known to us as John the Baptist. He was a Zealot, and
he announced in tirades all over the desert lands that those
who had submitted to Herod and to Rome were renegades and
heathen, living in defiance of the laws of Deuteronomy. This
meant, of course, all the rich and powerful among the Jews of
the time; it meant the Pharisees, Sadducees, and priests of the
Temple. He proclaimed the coming of a new leader, a stronger
one, a universal monarch who would be obeyed by all peoples
after they had submitted to baptism, the purification by water.

In answer to this announcement there had arisen no fewer
than three such would-be leaders. One was Judas of Galilee—
not that Judas Iscariot, whom we shall meet later in our story,
but the son of the old rebel Hizqiah. The second was a great
tall slave named Simon of Peraea, and the third was a still
more magnificent shepherd with the odd name of Athronga.
With the exception of Judas of Galilee, they were sons of the
common people, and they succeeded in raising a huge throng
of rebels from all over the land. They rushed upon Jerusalem,
laid siege to the Roman garrisons in Herod's palace and in
the forts. It was in this terrible struggle that the porticos of
the palace were burned. The slave Simon was killed, the magnificent Athronga was crucified with his three brothers, and
Judas of Galilee fled to the desert.

30

Ten years later he came out once more. That was the year before Yeshu had paid his boyhood visit to Jerusalem; he had
seen the wreckage of this attack, and heard the stories of it.

That time the rebels had seized the royal armories and obtained yeapons. Yet again Judas of Galilee had had to flee; and now the secret which was whispered to Yeshu by his tribe was that this man was hiding in the heavy bush which grew in the lower part of the Jordan valley near the Dead Sea; an outlaw, called by the Romans a bandit, but he was not that. He was a patriot, and Yeshu expressed a wish to meet him. His tribe took him to a lonely place, a hot place far below sea level, a home only for a man who loved freedom more than comfort. He and his followers were daggermen.

Here by a campfire Yeshu sat and talked with Judas. They were friends, but not allies, for in Yeshu's view the deliverance of his people was not to come by the swords of men but by the intervention of Adonai, who alone could bring the kingdom of righteousness upon earth. " 'Not by might nor by power, but by my spirit,' saith the Lord of hosts." This had been the message which the angel had brought to Zerubbabel during the building of the Temple in the days of the captivity in Babylon, and it fitted perfectly to the situation of the Hebrews under the captivity of Rome.

At least one of Yeshu's brothers, James, was to become a follower, first of Judas and then of Yeshu. He always deferred to Yeshu, recognizing the superiority of his mind; everyone who met him recognized that. He was an extraordinary man. Yeshu knew whole chapters of the Scriptures by heart, and was always ready with a text to answer one who opposed him. But he was mild in his arguments, never losing his temper except when he encountered deliberate falsehood or oppression. Then his wrath was terrible, and he went away and shook the dust of that man's place from his feet. He never left the Jewish lands, and knew only the country and the villages; but he knew the hearts and the history of his people, and his discourse was full of the stories of the ancient heroes and their dealings with their divine Protector.

Always he was seeking guidance from the Lord. It was his fate to live in the midst of failure; the dreams that he dreamed never came true, and the righteousness for which he yearned he was never permitted to see. Among individuals he might see it, among the lowly and the poor, who were kind to him, and understood his loving heart and cherished it; but never in public affairs, never among the rich and powerful, the so-called great. His native land was subject to the rule of an idolatrous and cruel empire. Jerusalem, his Holy City, was doomed to complete destruction within the time of those whom

Yeshu knew. The world of culture belonged to the Greeks, a finicking and decadent people whose educated classes thought much about the shaping of a verse but not much about righteousness and love.

Always and everywhere, Yeshu prayed for guidance. The Lord God would tell him how to save the chosen people—as He had told the prophets and the elect in times long past. The Lord would come Himself in His glory, or He would send a Messiah, an Anointed One, to rule over Israel, and drive out or destroy the alien hordes. God alone could do it, Elohim, the Heavenly Father who loved justice and mercy, and who heard the prayers of His true believers. He was the voice in Yeshu's soul; there He would speak, and when He spoke Yeshu would know His voice from the voice of any other in the world. He might even appear, as He had appeared to King Solomon of old, saying: "If my people, which are called by my name, shall humble themselves, and pray, and seek my face, and turn from their wicked ways; then will I hear from heaven, and will forgive their sin, and will heal their land."

Such was the promise which stood for a thousand years, and never had it crossed the mind of Yeshu the child or the youth that the promise would not be kept. Now it did not cross the mind of Yeshu the grown man.

31

In the year nineteen of what is now called the Christian era, this God-seeker was about twenty-six—for there appears to be good reason for thinking that he was born six or seven years prior to the time which Church authority in later years came to accept. Anyhow, what happened was that a new governor of Jerusalem was appointed by the Romans, an aristocrat named Pontius Pilate. He was a haughty man, and did not understand the Jews. Indeed, it was hard for a Roman gentleman to understand this fanatical people. He brought some of his troops into the castle which stood on the Temple hill; perhaps he did not think that this castle was sacred ground, but the Jews considered everything on that hill sacred. The troops set up their standard, which was something they carried as a symbol of their authority to rule in the Emperor's name. The standard was a pole with a base to keep it erect. At the top was a bronze tablet with a portrait of the Emperor in bas relief.

To the Jews this was a most frightful sacrilege; for, as we know, their first commandment, handed to Moses on tablets of stone, forbade the use of any kind of image. It was an especial outrage that the image of a living man should be set up inside the Temple of the most Holy God, a being so powerful that the Jews did not even risk speaking His name, but referred to him in various symbolical ways. There was a great uproar; the people of the nearby country came rushing into the city, and they all hastened to Pilate and begged him to remove the standards from the hill, "and to permit them to maintain the customs of their fathers." The Jewish historian Josephus tells us:

"When Pilate continued to decline their request, they fell on their faces and remained motionless for five days and nights. After that Pilate took his seat on the throne in the great hippodrome, and summoned the people, as though he intended to answer them, and he commanded the soldiers suddenly to surround the Jews in arms. When they saw the three bodies of troops surrounding them, they were sore afraid. And Pilate said to them menacingly: 'I shall cut you all down, if you will not admit Caesar's image.' Then he commanded the soldiers to draw their swords. But the Jews all with one consent fell down, extending their necks, exclaimed that they were ready like sheep for the slaughter rather than transgress the Law. Pilate, marveling at their fear of God and their purity, ordered the standards to be taken out of Jerusalem."

Doubtless he thought that would end the matter; but he did not know the Jews. The wildest excitement spread throughout the whole of Israel. There was weeping and wailing in all the synagogues, and the utmost terror as to what Shaddai the Terrible One would do to punish this unimaginable desecration of His holy Temple. Everyone took it as being the beginning of the fulfillment of that prophecy in the *Book of Daniel* concerning "the abomination that maketh desolation."

In the concluding three chapters of this *Book of Daniel* appears a confused set of prophecies having to do with the end of the world. In the third year of Cyrus, the king of Persia, there had come a vision to Daniel while he was by the side of a great river. An extraordinary man appeared before him, "his face as the appearance of lightning, and his eyes as lamps of fire." Daniel fell down upon his face in terror; the man told him to stand up, and the hand touched him and set him upon his knees and upon the palms of his hands. Then the man began to tell him all the calamities that were coming to the world.

Daniel was completely terrified, and again set his face to

the ground and exclaimed, "I have retained no strength. Or
how can the servant of this my Lord talk with this my Lord?
for as for me, straightway there remains no strength in me,
neither is there breath left in me." But the man went on and
told Daniel about the kings of the south, and the kings of the
north, and there would come "the abomination of desolation"
and after that there would be apparently only twelve hundred
and ninety days, or approximately three years and a half,
before the ending of the world.

"And at that time shall Michael stand up, the great prince
which standeth for the children of thy people: and there shall
be a time of trouble, such as never was since there was a nation
even to that same time: and at that time thy people shall be
delivered, every one that shall be found written in the book.
And many of them that sleep in the dust of the earth shall
awake, some to everlasting life, and some to shame and everlasting contempt. And they that be wise shall shine as the
brightness of the firmament; and they that turn many to
righteousness as the stars for ever and ever. But thou, O
Daniel, shut up the words, and seal the book, even to the time
of the end: many shall run to and fro, and knowledge shall be
increased." (DANIEL 12:1–4)

32

So there was tumult throughout all Israel and no way to stop
it. Proud Pilate must have been greatly disconcerted. It was
not merely weeping and wailing by the pious, and prophets
arising throughout all the land to make disturbances. It was
that still more dreadful thing which had happened a dozen
years ago, wild men arising in the deserts and coming forth
from the caves in the mountains to prophesy death and destruction, and to terrify the pious and cause them to run away
from Jerusalem and from the other towns, and flee to the wild
places, there secretly to arm themselves and prepare another
revolt to help the Lord in expelling the Romans and bringing
an end to the Roman empire.

Already there had passed a portion of the period allotted,
in which the faithful had a chance to make their escape. "And
whither did He lead them?" cried the preachers of this time.
"Some say, into the wilderness of Judah, and others say, into
the wilderness of Sihon and Og." Could any Roman gentleman
imagine anything more absurd? But in the brushland of that
lower Jordan valley, where the wild men had been hiding,
there arose the same Yohanan ben Zekharya, ex-priest—or

perhaps he was still a priest, for he had been chosen by the
rebels of twenty-three years ago, at the time of the death of
Herod and the terrible revolt of the Jews which had then
occurred. These wild men had made him their *meshuah
milhamah*, a sort of combination of high priest and army
chaplain, and he still held that position and filled that role,
and now he arose again to preach the abomination of desolation and the coming of the end of all things.

John the Baptist, as we call him, was now far past middle
years, with a long beard, and his hair was wild—it was a symbol of his power. This *barjona*, the "outside man," was dressed
in a camel's hair robe like the other Rechabites, and he was
barefoot. The rumors had it that he lived on locusts and wild
honey—a statement which has troubled the scholars. Some
think that the Greek word *akridas*, which means locusts, must
be a misprint for *akrides* which means the points or shoots of
plants. One scholar even suspects a jest by an enemy scribe
who turned the word *akrodrua* into *akridas*. *Akrodrua* means
tree fruits, and since this would include nuts, a man could
have got along very well on that diet. Many modern "health
cranks" do so—it is derisively known as the "squirrel diet."

But when one goes to the Jewish authorities one gets a new
point of view. Joseph Klausner tells us there are kinds of locusts which are clean, and others that are unclean; the clean
kind are pickled and eaten. The Bedouin Arabs are accustomed to boil locusts and eat them with salt, and during a
plague of locusts in modern Palestine (1917) the Yemenites
caught and ate them. The Baptist was an Essene, and not
supposed to eat flesh; but maybe locusts didn't count—we can
only guess.

Most educated Jews regarded Yohanan as a madman; but
there was much method in his madness. He believed in the
transmigration of souls, and his followers took up the idea
that he was a reincarnation of Elijah, the greatest of the
prophets. His camel's hair coat recalled the mantle of Elijah.
He lived in the Jordan wilderness where Elijah had lived, and
crossed the river at the very same ford. Elijah had been taken
up to heaven alive in a chariot of fire, and so had never known
death. He was believed to be the forerunner of the Messiah,
and if Yohanan was Elijah, that meant that the Messiah was
coming soon, and the prophecies of Daniel were actually about
to be fulfilled.

33

Also, every Jew remembered the words of Malachi, the last of
the prophets; words which Yohanan knew by heart. He was
another of those with proletarian sympathies. "Have we not
all one Father? Hath not one God created us? Why do we deal
treacherously every man against his brother, by profaning the
covenant of our fathers?" Like all the Hebrew prophets Malachi did not hesitate to speak in the name of the Lord. "Behold,
I will send my messenger, and he shall prepare the way before
me: and the Lord, whom ye seek, shall suddenly come to his
temple, even the messenger of the covenant, whom ye delight
in: behold, he shall come, saith the Lord of Hosts."

And he was going to be a terrible messenger, bringing destruction. "Who may abide the day of his coming? and who
shall stand when he appeareth? for he is like a refiner's fire."
All this fitted in with these terrible times, as you can see. Evil
ruled the land. "Ye have said, It is vain to serve God: and what
profit is it that we have kept His ordinance, and that we have
walked mournfully before the Lord of Hosts? And now we call
the proud happy; yea, they that work wickedness are set up;
yea, they that tempt God are even delivered."

Surely this was the time of Jerusalem under Pontius Pilate!
"For, behold, the day cometh, that shall burn as an oven; and
all the proud, yea, and all that do wickedly, shall be stubble:
and the day that cometh shall burn them up, saith the Lord
of hosts, that it shall leave them neither root nor branch."
Surely this meant the Romans and the faithless Jews who had
made terms with the Romans! The Jews who were holding to
the faith looked forward to the glorious days when they would
"tread down the wicked; for they shall be ashes under the soles
of your feet in the day I shall do this, saith the Lord God of
Hosts." The prophet went on to say, "Behold I shall send you
Elijah, the prophet before the coming of the great and dreadful day of the Lord."

Such was the promise, and now here was Elijah come back
to see that the promise was kept. Thousands of pious Jews
believed it, and came swarming from all over Palestine, listening to the word of the prophet and believing that the end was
at hand. It was to be the veritable and complete end this time.
"Repent ye, for the Kingdom of Heaven is at hand!"

"Kingdom of Heaven" was a Jewish phrase they used in
order to avoid speaking the name of the Most Holy One Himself. The Kingdom of Heaven meant the Kingdom of God, the

Messianic Age. The Talmud is full of the idea that if only the Jews would repent, the coming of this Kingdom would be at once. "Great is repentance which hastens the redemption." So Yohanan called upon the swarming people to repent of their sins, and as a symbol of this repentance he used upon them the ancient rite of baptism. He took them into the river and laid them down, and the water as a symbol washed their sins away; they arose new men, purified, as Josephus tells us, in both body and soul.

But when the Pharisees and Sadducees began coming to his baptism, John was not very cordial to them. "O generation of vipers, who hath warned you to flee from the wrath to come? Bring forth therefore fruits meet for repentance: and think not to say within yourselves, we have Abraham to our father: for I say unto you, that God is able of these stones to raise up children unto Abraham." This is a difficult saying, and people do not know what to make of it until they learn that it is a pun. The Gospels were written in Greek and the pun is not apparent in that language. In Hebrew the word for children is *banim* and the word for stones is *abanim*.

It might have been the old prophet Malachi speaking, when John continued, "And now also the ax is laid unto the root of the trees: therefore every tree which bringeth not forth good fruit is hewn down, and cast into the fire. I indeed baptize you with water unto repentance: but he that cometh after me is mightier than I, whose shoes I am not worthy to bear; he shall baptize you with the Holy Ghost, and with fire: whose fan is in his hand, and he will throughly purge his floor, and gather his wheat into the garner; but he will burn up the chaff with unquenchable fire."

The Christian commentators, of course, have taken this last as applying to their Christ. It is possible that the passage was interpolated in later years for that purpose. If Yohanan said it, he was talking about the Hebrew Messiah, the heavenly being who was coming to bring an end to the world and take the elect up to their reward. The four Gospels agree that John proclaimed Jesus as his Messiah; but it is permissible to regard this as an interpolation. It rarely happens that prophets, politicians, and other public figures who have grown old in the service of a cause, are eager to give up their authority to younger persons of untried ability. They hang onto their power, and have no difficulty in persuading themselves that they are the ones fitted to be trusted with command in the emergency which exists. Yohanan had been crying aloud in the

wilderness for a quarter century, and might be expected to
believe that the voice of the Lord was still calling him to this
service.

34

At this crisis the Spirit led Yeshu into the wilderness, and
there he fasted and prayed. At last he had got the guidance
he had been seeking. The time had come of which the prophets
had spoken, and for which the people had been waiting for a
thousand years. Yeshu perceived clearly what it was, and it
was not a Messiah King coming down from Heaven to restore
the Jewish people and build up their glory and power. No, it
was to be the end of the world—this world which the Lord had
created and which had so betrayed his hopes and purposes.
It was a world of wickedness and cruelty that could not be
worse; the patience of Adonai was exhausted, and the time of
judgment had come. Perhaps some day He would make a new
world, for with this one He was through. The ax would be laid
to the root of the trees; and Yeshu, who had cut down trees,
understood the meaning of this metaphor. There were some
kinds that if you left a little of the trunk it would send out
shoots again; but if you put the ax to the root, that would be
the end of any tree. Yohanan had said it, and he was the messenger, the new prophet of the end of all things. One thousand
two hundred and ninety days was the time specified by
Daniel, and already some of those days were gone, never to
return. Adonai would come in His dreadful Majesty, and
would scatter the wicked like chaff and burn them like fire.

What in the meantime did He want Yeshu to do? Surely
not to seek his own safety, to run away from the Lord of all
things. No, Yeshu must do what he could for those of his
people who still had some chance of salvation. He must go out
to them and preach repentance. He would raise his voice in
warning, and tell the story of the coming end of the world.
Again and again, Yeshu, with his arms upraised to the sky
and his frail body swaying with rhythmical ecstasy, asked the
Lord to tell him if this was right, if this was His will. Again
and again he felt in his soul those strange thrills, that hand as
it were lifting his spirit, those wings bearing him aloft. He
knew that this was the power of the Almighty, manifesting
itself within His mortal creature. He recalled words of the
prophet Isaiah which had worked in his soul since childhood.
"Also I heard the voice of the Lord, saying, 'Whom shall I

send, and who will go for us?' Then said I, 'Here am I; send me.' " (ISAIAH 6:8)

A terrible story was that! The Lord had bidden Isaiah to "make the heart of this people fat, and make their ears heavy, and shut their eyes; lest they see with their eyes, and hear with their ears, and understand with their heart, and convert, and be healed. Then said I, 'Lord, how long?' And he answered, 'Until the cities be wasted without inhabitant, and the houses without man, and the land be utterly desolate.' " (ISAIAH 6:10–11) Surely that time was come, and it would be that way with the land of Israel, and with all the lands of the Roman Empire! The Judgment day!

BOOK TWO

MISSION

❈　❈　❈

1

THE God-seeking man whose story we are following makes now his entrance upon the stage of history. He is young; we do not know exactly how young. We do not know the year of his birth; we do not know the year of his death; we do not know the date of any single event of his life. All that we have is a set of records, put down long afterwards, based upon tradition. The texts are highly suspect, and every statement must be critically examined, every word must be studied with care. All that an honest man can do is to make an estimate of probability, and remind you of this as he goes along.

The God-seeker's Hebrew name was Yeshu ben Yosef. The Romans called him Iesu, the I pronounced as y; in English his name is Jesus, and as we are writing English we now call him that. He was Jesus of Nazareth because he came from that small town of Galilee, and most probably was born there. The statement that he was born in Bethlehem I take to be a legend, created in order to fit him into an old prophecy that the Messiah would come from there. (MICAH 5:2) He was called the Nazarene because of his place of origin. There is another word, Nazarite, and the two words should be distinguished; a Nazarite, or Nasorite was a man who belonged to a peculiar sect, who did not drink wine, or cut his hair, or touch a corpse. It does not appear that Jesus was ever a Nazarite. He belonged to no sect.

The town of Nazareth was a market-place for the local farmers, and apparently of poor repute. A man named Nathanael hearing about Jesus inquired, "Can any good thing come out of Nazareth?"—a contemptuous question. There is still a town of Nazareth, and if you go there today, you will be shown the table at which Jesus sat, the bench at which he worked, the well from which he drank, and so on. The fact is that the old town was entirely destroyed, and the present town was perhaps built on a new and higher site. There is no

73

reason to think that there is any physical trace of Jesus in Palestine today; no more reason than there is for thinking that pieces of the "one true cross" in various shrines are genuine.

He came back from the river Jordan into Galilee, and began to preach repentance in preparation for the coming Kingdom of God, or for the end of the world. He probably did not baptize anyone, or tell his disciples to do so. The John Gospel says he did, but for reasons to be stated later I do not consider this Gospel to carry much weight.

"Worship the Father in spirit and in truth," was his command. He was a man of the spirit, a preacher of righteousness, and he practised what he preached. His sexual life was blameless, we may be sure, for he made a great number of enemies, and they have continued to fight him down through the ages; if there had been any scandals about him, these would have appeared in the tradition. The Jews of a later time called him Yeshu ben Pantera, which means 'son of the Panther.' They invented a legendary Roman soldier named Pantera who, they said, had seduced his mother. Just so in our day malicious tales are made up concerning public persons.

The worst that could be said about him was that while he preached love, he sometimes became irritated and used bitter language; that, and the fact that he disregarded the Sabbath, so important to the Jews. He had the worship and the love of God guiding him and determining the whole of his life. He had no other idea and no other interest; nothing was important, compared with the wonder and righteousness of God, whom he referred to as his "Heavenly Father." God had created this world in six days, and He might destroy it all in six seconds, and the only thing of consequence was that you should believe in Him, honor Him, obey Him, in order that in the Day of Judgment you would be among those who were selected for immortality in His eternal dwelling place. And never must you seek this goal for yourself alone; love of man followed automatically from love of God.

In setting out to tell this story a writer has two choices: he can paraphrase it, or he can pick out such passages from the New Testament as suit his purpose. I have declined the former program, because I have no consciousness of ability to improve upon the ancient texts. I have preferred the authorized or "King James" version because I was brought up on it, and such quaintness of style as I find in it is a part of its atmosphere and charm. I have preferred the Mark story as a rule, because it is more factual and simple, with the least amount of doctrine. My story is a series of quotes, with comment and interpretation which you, the reader, may judge, and accept if you find it worthy. There are millions of persons in this country who have never opened a Bible, and for whom the story will be a novelty.

Mark tells us, "Jesus came into Galilee, preaching the gospel of the kingdom of God, and saying, 'The time is fulfilled, and the kingdom of God is at hand: repent ye, and believe the Gospel.'" (MARK 1:14–15) The English word 'gospel' is derived from the Anglo-Saxon 'godspell.' The word which Jesus used, or which Mark or someone used for him, was the Greek word *evangelion*, and both words mean good tidings. The good tidings which Jesus was telling was that the Lord was coming down from heaven to deliver his people, and that every Jew who would repent of his sins and put his trust in Him would be saved.

2

The story continues: "Now as he walked by the sea of Galilee, he saw Simon and Andrew his brother casting a net into the sea: for they were fishers. And Jesus said unto them, 'Come ye after me, and I will make you become fishers of men'; and straightway they forsook their nets, and followed him." These words are interesting, as showing how completely the mind of Jesus was saturated with the ideas and language of the ancient prophets. He is here referring to a passage from the sixteenth chapter of Jeremiah, in which this prophet of six centuries before him was threatening the sinful Hebrews with the wrath of their jealous God. "Behold I will send for many fishers, saith the Lord, and they shall fish them; and after will I send for many hunters, and they shall hunt them from every mountain, and from every hill, and out of the holes of the rocks: for mine eyes are upon all their ways: they are not hid from my face, neither is their iniquity hid from mine eyes." (JEREMIAH 16:16–17)

Jesus at the outset of his mission presumably chose humble fishermen because they were his kind of people. Their minds were not troubled by the sophistications which men acquire in towns. They were ready to believe what he told them, and to believe it so thoroughly that they would leave all and follow him.

"And when he had gone a little farther thence, he saw James the son of Zebedee, and John his brother, who also were in the ship mending their nets. And straightway he called them: and they left their father Zebedee in the ship with the hired servants, and went after him. And they went into Capernaum; and straightway on the Sabbath day he entered into the synagogue, and taught. And they were astonished at his doctrine: for he taught them as one who had authority, and not as the scribes. And there was in their synagogue a man with an unclean spirit; and he cried out, saying, 'Let us alone; what have we to do with thee, thou Jesus of Nazareth? art thou come to destroy us? I know thee who thou art, the Holy One of God.' And Jesus rebuked him, saying, 'Hold thy peace, and come out of him.' And when the unclean spirit had torn him, and cried with a loud voice, he came out of him. And they were all amazed, insomuch that they questioned among themselves, saying, 'What thing is this? What new doctrine is this? For with authority commandeth he even the unclean spirits, and they do obey him.' And immediately his fame spread abroad throughout all the region round about Galilee." (MARK 1:19–28)

3

So here we have the first of Jesus' miracles. It has been my promise to avoid controversy in this portion of the story, but there is no use going on without discussing this question of miracles; for his ministry, which lasted a year or two, is a succession of them, and we have to come to some agreement on the subject. What this writer believes is that some kinds of "miracles" happen and some kinds don't. I do not believe that Jesus ever walked on the Lake of Galilee, or fed five thousand with a few loaves and fishes, or raised Lazarus after he had been buried four days in the earth. But I have no difficulty in believing that he healed many sick persons, and cast out many "unclean spirits."

What did the ancient Hebrews mean when they said that a man had an unclean or evil spirit? They meant that he was insane. If the man himself believed in evil spirits, his delusions would take the form of being possessed by such spirits. Had he lived in modern times, and was taken to a psychiatrist, the psychiatrist would say that he had an obsession, or a schizoid personality, or some such expensive affliction.

Let us take a modern case, a classic in its field. Dr. Morton Prince was one of the most eminent psychologists of the past generation, editor of the *Journal of Abnormal Psychology*, and Professor of Nervous Diseases at Tufts College Medical

School. He gave to this case an entire book, called *The Dissociation of a Personality*. For many years he treated a young lady of Boston who suffered from possession by several different personalities; he sorted them out and identified five. The young lady would go to sleep as one personality and wake up as another. Some of these personalities knew one another, others didn't.

One of them, whom Dr. Prince named Sally, was to all intents and purposes what the Bible calls an unclean spirit, or demon. Of course if you don't like these words, you can call her a polymorphous-perverse psychic entity, or just a hateful character, or whatever label seems to you least suggestive of superstition. Sally would come into possession of Miss Beauchamp's mind, her body, and all her belongings, and would take delight in making trouble for the other personalities, whom she knew and ridiculed to Dr. Prince. Miss Beauchamp would set out on a trip, and on the way Sally would take possession of her and spend all her money, leaving her stranded and not knowing how she had got there. Sally would tell Dr. Prince about it with malicious glee.

Dr. Prince was treating the case by hypnosis, and these various personalities would come to the surface at his command, and when he questioned them, they would talk with him and tell him about themselves. He continued the treatment for years, giving suggestions to the various personalities; he combined two of the best and made them into a new Miss Beauchamp. As for Sally, what he did was to murder her— that is, psychiatrically speaking; he told her that she would no longer exist, that she would go away and leave Miss Beauchamp alone, and she did so. As you see, here was a most eminent Boston psychologist 'casting out' an 'unclean spirit.' The only difference was the length of time required and the set of ideas used in the cure.

The last time I met Dr. Prince, shortly before his death, I asked him about Miss Beauchamp, and he told me that she had been and was living a perfectly normal life. She had been completely cured by suggestion. I don't know whether her healer believed in God or not, but I am sure that he would have agreed that God is a powerful suggestion. Sometimes this powerful suggestion has been able to make cures in a few seconds which might take a patient psychiatrist years to effect.

4

I want to make it possible for modern men and women to read about Jesus with understanding and sympathy, and without parting with their common sense. More and more medical men are coming to realize the effect of mind upon the body, and to recognize that there are many afflictions, to all appearances physical, which are of mental origin. They have even invented a new and entirely respectable term for these problems; they talk about 'psychosomatic medicine.' Some of them welcome religious help in such cases, and others wish they could. With the idea of helping along that important idea, I am going to tell briefly three family stories about "miracles." Obviously, they have nothing to do with the story of Jesus; but they have something to do with what we believe about it.

Some twenty years ago, after a period of overwork and strain, I was seized with a spell of what the doctors called double hiccoughs, lasting for three days and nights without a moment's letup. I was completely exhausted, my heart was failing, and the eminent physician and surgeon of Pasadena who was attending me called an ambulance and told my wife that he would have to put me under an oxygen tent. My wife, being frantic, ran to the telephone and looked up the name of a Christian Science practitioner and called this woman, whose name she had never heard before. The woman came into the room, and I barely remember her coming; I was so close to unconsciousness that I only knew she was telling me that I would stop hiccoughing. She said a few words about God being present and that He would help me; my hiccoughs ceased, and I fell asleep, and when I woke up again I was ready to take some food. I have never had a return of the hiccoughs since that time. The doctor, who walked off the case when the Christian Science lady came in, afterwards told my wife that he would forgive her!

Second, my wife herself: through overwork and worry she brought upon herself in middle age a severe case of varicose veins in the legs. The veins were swollen and dark purple. The same physician of Pasadena, head of the great hospital and a high-ranking army surgeon in World War I, declared that they would have to be operated on, and that my wife would have to wear rubber stockings for the rest of her days.

She had been investigating the subject of mental healing, and there had come to this country a friendly little gentleman named Emile Coué, who treated sick people by teaching them to repeat over and over to themselves the formula: "Day by day in every way I am getting better and better." The sophisticates of New York, who think that Freud discovered the subconscious mind and that he discovered in it nothing but evil, considered Coué the joke of the season and made all kinds of fun of him. The present writer, who had been reading about the subconscious mind from his youth up, met Coué in New York, appeared on the platform with him, and told of cures by suggestion and autosuggestion of which he had knowledge. My wife decided to try this method, and did so persistently. In a few weeks every trace of the swelling and discoloration of the veins had disappeared. She has been active and well ever since that time, about thirty years ago.

Third, my wife's mother, a devoutly religious lady of Mississippi, who had six sons. One of them, as a small child, developed tuberculosis of the hip, and the mother took him to Chicago to a then-famous Dr. Murphy, who declared that an operation was required, and that the child would be a cripple for life. When the mother announced that she was going to pray for the child, the doctor said that this could do no harm, but that she should not delay about it; the operation was imperative. She took the child home and prayed over him day and night, and in a few weeks every trace of the trouble disappeared. She took him back to Dr. Murphy and he said these precise words: "It is a miracle." I know that it sounds melodramatic, but I tell it because it is true; this child grew up to be six-feet-four and a famous football player on the team of Alabama University; his name appeared on the so-called 'All-America team.' When he came home from college he was so happy to see his mother that he caught her in his arms and gave her a hug and broke three of her ribs. All this she told me herself, and I can assure you that she was a most truthful person.

5

These are family stories, and you do not know the family. It will be more to the point to cite a medical authority, one of the greatest of recent times. Religious healings are reported continually from the Roman Catholic shrine at Lourdes, on the French side of the Pyrenees mountains. There is a medical bureau there, for the study of these phenomena, and among the physicians who went there and studied the cases and the reports was Dr. Alexis Carrel, who in 1912 received the Nobel Prize "for work on vascular ligature and grafting of blood vessels and organs." Dr. Carrel was brought up as a Catholic, but left the Church early. For many years he was at the Rockefeller Institute, and became known to the newspapers because he cultivated a piece of chicken heart in a solution in order to prove the immortality of the cell. This piece of heart grew indefinitely and is still growing. Every so often the greater part has to be cut away, otherwise there would be no room for anything in the Institute but chicken-heart tissue. He and Charles Lindbergh constructed an artificial heart for use in certain surgical cases. No one can question his competence as a scientific observer.

Carrel satisfied himself that some of the "miracles" at Lourdes were genuine, and in his wise book called *Man the Unknown*, published in 1935, he deals with the cases in detail. He says: "In all countries, at all times, people have believed in the existence of miracles, in the more or less rapid healing of the sick at places of pilgrimage, at certain sanctuaries. But after the great impetus of science during the nineteenth century, such belief completely disappeared. It was generally admitted, not merely that miracles did not exist, but that they could not exist. As the laws of thermodynamics make perpetual motion impossible, physiological laws oppose miracles. Such is still the attitude of most physiologists and physicians. However, in view of the facts observed during the last fifty years this attitude cannot be sustained. The most important cases of miraculous healing have been recorded by the Medical Bureau of Lourdes. Our present conception of the influence of prayer upon pathological lesions is based upon the observation of patients who have been cured almost instantaneously of various afflictions, such as peritoneal tuberculosis, cold abscesses, ostoitis, suppurating wounds, lupus, cancer, etc. The process of healing changes little from one individual to another. Often, an acute pain. Then a sudden sensation of being cured. In a few seconds, a few minutes, at the most a few hours, wounds are cicatrized, pathological symptoms disappear, appetite returns. Some times functional disorders vanish before the anatomical lesions are repaired. The skeletal deformations of Pott's disease, the cancerous glands, may still persist two or three days after the healing of the main lesions. The miracle is chiefly characterized by an extreme acceleration of the processes of organic repair. There is no doubt that the rate of cicatrization of the anatomical defects is much greater than the normal one. The only condition indispensable to the occurrence of the phenomenon is prayer. But there is no need for the patient himself to pray, or even to have any religious faith. It is sufficient that some one around him be in a state of prayer. Such facts are of profound significance. They show the reality of certain relations, of still unknown nature, between psychological and organic processes. They prove the objective importance of the spiritual activities, which hygienists, physicians, educators and sociologists have almost always neglected to study. They open to man a new world."

Man should enter that world without delay.

6

Such cures have been made throughout history, and they are being made all over the world today by Christian Scientists, Catholics, Hindu Yogis, and perhaps even by African witch doctors. We say that they are due to suggestions given to the subconscious mind. That comforts us, and we overlook the fact that we don't know what the subconscious mind is and find great difficulty in imagining mind without consciousness. The truth is that we are only at the beginning of finding out about our own minds. We don't know how they come into existence; we don't know how they work; we don't know what are the forces which guide and sustain them; we don't know whether our subconscious mind is really sub or super—that is, whether it comes out of our animal being, or is a part of God, or both.

This much we do know: there is something in us that creates us and sustains us, that understands the pattern of our being, and knows how to repair the damage that may be done to us. If we cut a hole in our finger, we don't expect to have a hole in our finger for the rest of our lives. We expect that some mysterious power will send blood to that place and sort out the various materials to make the various kinds of tissue that belong in that place. We expect that this "miracle" will happen of itself; but it seems to me that the sorting out of materials is an act of mind and does not happen of itself or by accident. The doctors call this force *vis medicatrix naturae:* Bernard Shaw called it the life forces, the French philosopher Bergson called it the *élan vitale,* the American Emerson called it the Oversoul. Jesus called it God, which is a shorter word and easier to say, but no easier to understand. My wife, who has gone into the subject more deeply than I, bids me say that it is intense concentration which brings the results; and, of course, it is easier to concentrate upon the idea that God is helping you to do so.

You will note in the story which you have just read about Jesus in the synagogue that the unclean spirit cried out, "I know thee who thou art, the holy one of God." It may be that the unclean spirit said those words, but it seems more likely that they were put into the text when the story was first written, or when it was copied and recopied in the scriptoria where manuscripts were made. It is a pious statement, and fits in with the conception of Jesus which quickly began to spread after his death. I quote it in order to show how, in reading these Gospel texts, we have to bear in mind the operations of pious interpolators. Some episode may bear the stamp of genuineness, and only one word, or one sentence, or one verse may be suspect. There is no way to be certain, and every person has to set up his own criteria. Let him do this humbly and earnestly; as a lover of truth.

7

Jesus became a famous wonder worker; and it was a great annoyance to him. They brought him the sick, and because he was filled with pity for their need he healed them. The crowds followed him, and when he went into the desert to pray his disciples came to him and told him that the people were waiting for him. "And at even, when the sun did set, they brought unto him all that were diseased, and them that were possessed with devils." (MARK 1:32) He healed a leper and told the man not to say anything about it; "but the man went out, and began to publish it much, and to blaze abroad the matter, insomuch that Jesus could no more openly enter into the city, but was without in desert places: and they came to him from every quarter." (MARK 1:45) There is nothing unlikely about all this; the same things happened to a faith healer who came to California from Iran a few years ago.

A little later, we are told that "the unclean spirits, when they saw him, fell down before him, and cried, saying, 'Thou art the Son of God.' And he straitly charged them that they should not make him known." How the spirits knew him, and why he wanted to keep this secret, I leave to the theologians. My own belief is that Jesus, a good and pious Jew, wanted nothing to do with demigods, or with the demigod beliefs of Romans, Greeks, Syrians, Persians or Egyptians; they were all around him, and he considered them beneath his notice.

The subject came up again when the little group visited the towns of Caesarea Philippi in Syria "And by the way he asked his disciples, saying unto them, 'Whom do men say that

I am?' And they answered, 'John the Baptist': but some say
'Elias'; and others, 'One of the prophets.' And he saith unto
them, 'But whom say ye that I am?' And Peter answereth and
saith unto him, 'Thou art the Christ.' And he charged them
that they should tell no man of him. And he began to teach
them, that the son of man must suffer many things, and be rejected of the elders, and of the chief priests, and scribes, and
be killed, and after three days rise again. And he spake that
saying openly. And Peter took him, and began to rebuke him;
but when he had turned about and looked on his disciples, he
rebuked Peter saying, 'Get thee behind me, Satan: for thou
savourest not the things that be of God, but the things that
be of men.' And when he had called the people unto him with
his disciples also, he said unto them, 'Whosoever will come
after me, let him deny himself, and take up his cross, and follow me. For whosoever will save his life shall lose it; but whosoever shall lose his life for my sake and the Gospel's, the same
shall save it. For what shall it profit a man, if he shall gain
the whole world, and lose his own soul? Or what shall a man
give in exchange for his soul? Whosoever therefore shall be
ashamed of me and of my words in this adulterous and sinful
generation; of him also shall the Son of man be ashamed, when
he cometh in the glory of his Father with the holy angels.' "
(MARK 8:27–38)

Here again we have the problem of textual changes. It is
possible that the word "Christ" may have been spoken; for, as
we have seen, it does not mean Son of God, but Anointed One,
and it is conceivable that Jesus may have decided that he had
received a commission from on high. But the last sentence I
take to be interpolated; I believe that any sentence in which
Jesus accepts the idea that he is God is an interpolation of
Christian zealotry. Jesus himself not only did not think that
he was God; he did not think that he was even good. He rebuked a man for addressing him as "good Master" and replied, "Why callest thou me good? there is none good but one,
that is, God." This is in the story of the rich young man who
was told to keep the commandments; and when he said he had
done that, he was told to sell all that he had and give to the
poor and then follow Jesus; "he went away sorrowful, for he
had great possessions." (MATTHEW 19:16–24)

The present monotheistic writer is not so naive as to hope
that Christian devotees will pay serious attention to a passage
telling them that God alone is good. It has stood for eighteen
centuries or more and not many devotees have heeded it. The

surprising thing is that the remark was allowed to stand, instead of being cut out as heresy. To me in my student years it was an important text, because it helped to set my mind free from superstition. As an example of what I mean I cite the verse from Mark: "And he began to teach them, that the Son of man must suffer many things, and be rejected of the elders, and of the chief priests, and scribes, and be killed, and after three days rise again." (MARK 8:31) This, according to the pious, constitutes a prophecy. To me it is something which a Church Father of the first or second century composed with the noblest of intentions.

8

This episode of Caesarea Philippi concludes with another highly controversial statement as follows: "Verily I say unto you, that there be some of them that stand here, which shall not taste of death, till they have seen the kingdom of God come with power." (MARK 9:1)

And what are we to make of that? Is it an interpolation? It can hardly be, because when the Christian traditions were put into writing in their present form, the persons who had known Jesus were long since dead and it was evident that this prophecy had not come true. Why then did not some pious scribe cut it out? Perhaps it was too menacing; if the Kingdom of God should come the next day, what would happen to one who had just been guilty of mutilating the most important prophecy of the Son of God? The same statement appears in all three of the so-called Synoptics, that is, Matthew, Mark and Luke. "Verily I say unto you, that this generation shall not pass, till all these things be done."

This aspect of the life and teaching of Jesus is crucial, and until quite recent times has been pretty well neglected by Christian commentators—except the Seventh-Day Adventists and other millennial sects. No story of Jesus is complete, or indeed makes sense at all, without giving due weight to this aspect of his faith and utterance. That he meant it literally I have no slightest doubt.

9

It is time to consult the other Gospels and see what they have to tell us about Jesus. They contain many more anecdotes and many more sayings—for the narrative of Mark is rather bare. Matthew was the one who put in the sermons and doctrines, while Luke gives the poetry and the literary touches. Matthew tells how Jesus was "led up of the spirit into the wilderness to be tempted of the devil." This story of the temptation of the Son of God, who was a part of the Trinity and therefore God himself, is interesting as poetry and legend; but taken literally, as believers take it, it seems to me meaningless. If God is all, and knows all, I do not see how He can be tempted; but that does not weaken the importance of the words which Jesus spoke to the devil, "Man shall not live by bread alone."

Multitudes began to follow Jesus, and he opened his mouth and taught them the famous *Beatitudes:*

"Blessed are the poor in spirit: for theirs is the kingdom of heaven; blessed are they that mourn: for they shall be comforted; blessed are the meek: for they shall inherit the earth; blessed are they which do hunger and thirst after righteousness: for they shall be filled; blessed are the merciful: for they shall obtain mercy; blessed are the pure in heart: for they shall see God; blessed are the peacemakers: for they shall be called the children of God; blessed are they which are persecuted for righteousness' sake: for theirs is the kingdom of heaven; blessed are ye, when men shall revile you, and persecute you, and shall say all manner of evil against you falsely, for my sake; rejoice, and be exceeding glad: for great is your reward in heaven: for so persecuted they the prophets which were before you." (MATTHEW 5:3–12)

These sayings are the heart of the ethical teaching of Jesus, and have made him the friend of all mankind. Few of them are original, in the sense that nothing like them had been said before; on the contrary, Jewish scholars have taken the *Sermon on the Mount* sentence by sentence and shown that equivalent statements have been made in the Old Testament, and in the *Book of Ben Sira* and other volumes of their literature prior to the time of Jesus. But the sayings as a whole reveal a point of view and a personality; a man of insight and force, a man of spiritual vision and an extraordinary gift of expression. Here, as everywhere, we have to be on the alert to detect passages which have nothing to do with the historical Jesus, but are part of the legend which was built up about him after his death. When he draws a picture of himself sitting at the right hand of his Father, judging the just and unjust who come before him and deciding their destinies, I venture to guess that this is an insertion of many years later.

10

What we know and recognize and love is the teacher of righteousness here on earth; of justice, mercy and kindness among men. He tells his Jewish 'multitude': "Ye are the salt of the earth: but if the salt have lost his savour, wherewith shall it be salted? it is thenceforth good for nothing, but to be cast out, and to be trodden under foot of men. Ye are the light of the world. A city that is set on an hill cannot be hid. Neither do men light a candle, and put it under a bushel, but on a candlestick; and it giveth light unto all that are in the house. Let your light so shine before men, that they may see your good works, and glorify your Father which is in heaven." (MATTHEW 5:13–16)

He forbids revenge in any form, or any punishment: "Ye have heard that it hath been said, an eye for an eye, and a tooth for a tooth; but I say unto you, that ye resist not evil: but whosoever shall smite thee on thy right cheek, turn to him the other also. And if any man will sue thee at the law, and take away thy coat, let him have thy cloke also. And whosoever shall compel thee to go a mile, go with him twain. Give to him that asketh thee, and from him that would borrow of thee turn not thou away." (MATTHEW 5:38–42)

In certain passages he seems to impose upon them not merely absolute pacifism, but absolute non-resistance of any sort; exactly what his desert tribe had been practising for centuries. "Ye have heard that it was said by them of old time, thou shalt not kill; and whosoever shall kill shall be in danger of the judgment; but I say unto you, that whosoever is angry with his brother without a cause shall be in danger of the judgment: and whosoever shall say to his brother, Raca, shall be in danger of the council: but whosoever shall say, thou fool, shall be in danger of hell fire. Therefore if thou bring thy gift to the altar, and there rememberest that thy brother hath ought against thee; leave there thy gift before the altar, and go thy way; first be reconciled to thy brother, and then come and offer thy gift." (MATTHEW 5:21–24)

He forbids hatred of enemies: "Ye have heard that it hath been said, thou shalt love thy neighbour, and hate thine enemy. But I say unto you, love your enemies, bless them that curse you, do good to them that hate you, and pray for them which despitefully use you, and persecute you; that ye may be the children of your Father which is in heaven: for He maketh His sun to rise on the evil and on the good, and sendeth rain on the just and on the unjust. For if ye love them which love you, what reward have ye? do not even the publicans the same? And if ye salute your brethren only, what do ye more than others? do not even the publicans so? Be ye therefore perfect, even as your Father which is in heaven is perfect." (MATTHEW 5:43–48)

All these are hard sayings. They were adapted to the life of the desert, but surely not to the business life of Jerusalem, any more than to the business life of today. There are millions who call themselves Christians who go to church on Sunday and listen to these words, but on Monday morning they manifest no consciousness of having heard them, and if you were to remind them of the words, they would set you down for an odd character.

11

The little child who went to Jerusalem has now become a man. He has not forgotten what he saw there; he has reflected on it and understands it thoroughly. He now warns against pride and pomp, and you can see in every word that he is thinking about the scribes and Pharisees whom he watched in Jerusalem and in Galilee. "Take heed that ye do not your alms before men, to be seen of them: otherwise ye have no reward of your Father which is in heaven. Therefore when thou doest thine alms, do not sound a trumpet before thee, as the hypocrites do in the synagogues and in the streets, that they may have glory of men. Verily I say unto you, they have their reward. But when thou doest alms, let not thy left hand know what thy right hand doeth; that thine alms may be in secret: and thy Father which seeth in secret himself shall reward thee openly. And when thou prayest, thou shalt not be as the hypocrites are: for they love to pray standing in the synagogues and in the corners of the streets, that they may be seen of men. Verily I say unto you, they have their reward. But thou, when thou prayest, enter into thy closet, and when thou hast shut thy door, pray to thy Father which is in secret; and thy Father which seeth in secret shall reward thee openly. But when ye pray, use not vain repetitions, as the heathen do; for they think that they shall be heard for their much speaking. Be not ye therefore like unto them: for your Father knoweth what things ye have need of, before ye ask Him." (MATTHEW 6:1–8)

In order that there may be no mistake about it he tells the

people exactly how to pray. He suggests a prayer for them, which has come to be known as *The Lord's Prayer,* and has been repeated throughout Christendom ever since. If we study this text phrase by phrase, we perceive Jesus in it, and we do not have to be troubled by the idea of some scholars that it was put together later by some follower. Whoever it was, he had learned the great teacher's mind. Let us do the same:

"Our Father which art in Heaven": this, as we know, is the basic fact of the universe as Jesus sees it. "Hallowed be thy name": this is the purpose for which Jesus lives, and for which he advises you and me to live. "Thy Kingdom come": the future as he sees it, and the goal upon which all eyes must be centered. "Thy will be done on earth, as it is in Heaven": this is, in his view, the heart of all religion and all morals. "Give us this day our daily bread": this is economics as he sees it; we do not get our daily bread, but God gives it to us. "And forgive us our debts, as we forgive our debtors": in some of the translations this is rendered "forgive us our trespasses, as we forgive those who trespass against us." This may be intended to be more helpful to the business world, but it comes to the same thing in the end; we must wipe out the evils of the past, and start all over in a righteous present, looking forward to a blessed future. "And lead us not into temptation, but deliver us from evil": temptation and evil besiege us at every moment of our life in this world, and the only way we can escape them is to have the presence of God in our hearts; to be instantly aware of Him and of His operation within us. "For Thine is the Kingdom, and the Power, and the Glory for ever. Amen." This last requires no comment, being the same as the opening sentence, "Hallowed be Thy name."

This prayer represents the complete absorption of the individual in the idea of his Creator, in the contemplation of the Creator and the absoluteness of the Creator's perfection. From first to last Jesus is a man of absolutes; he makes few compromises with the world and its standards. Our earthly standards are of no consequence, because we are on our way to heaven, and our only care must be to get there. But notice, he does not anywhere say 'me' and 'mine'; he says 'us' and 'our.' The Lord's Prayer is collective, and we, the petitioners, must be exactly as much concerned to help our neighbors get to heaven as we are to get ourselves there. Jesus goes on immediately to say: "For if ye forgive men their trespasses, your heavenly Father will also forgive you; but if ye forgive not men their trespasses, neither will your Father forgive your trespasses." (MATTHEW 6:14–15) We are all God's children, and we are all one in His sight, and all equal.

12

The teacher goes on to command: "Lay not up for yourselves treasures upon earth, where moth and rust doth corrupt, and where thieves break through and steal; but lay up for yourselves treasures in heaven, where neither moth nor rust doth corrupt, and where thieves do not break through nor steal; for where your treasure is, there will your heart be also." (MATTHEW 6:19–21)

This, you perceive, is another hard saying. Impossible to imagine a statement more explicit, or more horrifying to the average man of this world. If you have been startled by my portrayal of Jesus as a man of the desert, you should be convinced by reading these sentences; for it is a desert man speaking, a Rechabite man who has no property, and cares nothing for property, but all his life has traveled from place to place, getting his daily bread with the help of God, and having no possessions that he cannot carry upon his back— even though it may be a bent back.

"No man can serve two masters: for either he will hate the one, and love the other; or else he will hold to the one, and despise the other. Ye cannot serve God and mammon. Therefore I say unto you, Take no thought for your life, what ye shall eat, or what ye shall drink; nor yet for your body, what ye shall put on. Is not the life more than meat, and the body than raiment? Behold the fowls of the air; for they sow not, neither do they reap, nor gather into barns; yet our heavenly Father feedeth them. Are ye not much better than they? Which of you by taking thought can add one cubit unto his stature? And why take ye thought for raiment? Consider the lilies of the field, how they grow; they toil not, neither do they spin; and yet I say unto you, That even Solomon in all his glory was not arrayed like one of these. Wherefore, if God so clothe the grass of the field, which to day is, and tomorrow is cast into the oven, shall he not much more clothe you, O ye of little faith? But seek ye first the kingdom of God, and His righteousness and all these things shall be added unto you." (MATTHEW 6:24–30; 33)

It seems to this present commentator clear that the above injunctions could hardly have been issued by a man raised in Galilee; for Galilee was a farming country, and every farmer

in the world knows that you have to take thought for the mor-
row, and take it continually. The farmer knows that human
beings are not fed like the fowls of the air. A farmer has cattle, or at least one cow, or one or two goats, and the farmer
knows that these creatures have to be fed and have to be
milked twice a day. A farmer knows that the soil has to be
prepared and the weather watched. He knows that seeds have
to be selected and that weeds have to be destroyed. He knows
that the harvest has to be gathered, and food preserved for
the winter season, or his family will starve. It is only the
desert man who can take nature as he finds it; who knows
that edible roots grow of themselves, and that rabbits start
up from under bushes and can be knocked over with a
crooked throw stick. It is only the wandering artisan who
knows that he can always come into the farming country
and find some peasant who will give him food in return for
labor.

13

What is to be noted about these moral sayings is their extraordinary force and compactness. Every sentence is like a
hammer blow, and I doubt if anywhere in the world's literature you can find such a series of quotations and familiar
similes as in this wonderful Sermon on the Mount. Take, for
example, the following eight verses, which constitute *Matthew
7:13–20.* Not a line that is not known to literate people all
over the world—and not merely Christian believers, but
readers of literature, and those who think about life.

"Enter ye in at the strait gate: for wide is the gate, and
broad is the way, that leadeth to destruction, and many there
be which go in thereat: because strait is the gate, and narrow
is the way, which leadeth unto life, and few there be that find
it. Beware of false prophets, which come to you in sheep's
clothing, but inwardly they are ravening wolves. Ye shall
know them by their fruits. Do men gather grapes of thorns,
or figs of thistles? Even so every good tree bringeth forth
good fruit; but a corrupt tree bringeth forth evil fruit. Every
tree that bringeth not forth good fruit is hewn down, and
cast into the fire. Wherefore by their fruits ye shall know
them."

Also, the man has a tongue like a whip-lash. He preaches
brotherhood and love, but coupled with burning moral in-
dignation. He does not suffer fools gladly. "And one of the
company said unto him, Master, speak to my brother, that he

divide the inheritance with me. And he said unto him, 'Man,
who made me a judge or a divider over you?'" (LUKE
12:13–14) Then he takes the occasion to give his customary
Rechabite advice: "He said unto them, take heed, and beware
of covetousness; for a man's life consisteth not in the abundance of the things which he possesseth." (LUKE 12:15)

14

He has forbidden to call a man a fool; but he himself does
not hesitate to do it when he is aroused. His denunciations of
the Pharisees are cruel, and not entirely deserved, for many
of them were earnest men, striving for goodness as they saw
it, but tied in the bonds of an outworn creed. They had
achieved an intellectual conquest, not merely of Judea, but
of all Palestine; and here came this wild man, unlettered and
uncouth, condemning and abusing! It is worth noting that
Jesus is more bitter against the scribes and Pharisees in the
Matthew and Luke Gospels than in Mark; which may be
because at the time the earlier Gospel was written, the
Christians and the Jews had not split so far apart. Jesus was
a Jew; and the men who put the Matthew and Luke stories
together in the Greek language may have been gentiles, or
gentile-minded.

Jesus was the poor man who had earned bread by the
sweat of his brow, and who, wherever he went among men,
was confronted by the spectacle of ill-gotten wealth vaunting
its power. He was invited to share these privileges, and sometimes did so, but even then did not consider it necessary to
be conventionally polite; he broke all the rules of social hospitality, and delivered a long tirade to his hosts.

"And as he spake, a certain Pharisee besought him to dine
with him: and he went in, and sat down to meat. And when
the Pharisee saw it he marvelled that he had not first washed
before dinner. And the Lord said unto him, 'Now do ye Pharisees make clean the outside of the cup and the platter; but
your inward part is full of ravening and wickedness. Ye fools,
did not He that made that which is without make that which
is within also? But rather give alms of such things as ye
have; and, behold, all things are clean unto you. But woe
unto you, Pharisees! for ye love the uppermost seats in the
synagogues, and greetings in the markets. Woe unto you,
scribes and Pharisees, hypocrites! for ye are as graves which
appear not, and the men that walk over them are not aware
of them.' Then answered one of the lawyers, and said unto

him, 'Master, thus saying thou reproachest us also.' And he said, 'Woe unto you also, ye lawyers! for ye lade men with burdens grievous to be borne, and ye yourselves touch not the burdens with one of your fingers. Woe unto you! for ye build the sepulchres of the prophets, and your fathers killed them. Truly ye bear witness that ye allow the deeds of your fathers: for they indeed killed them, and ye build their sepulchres. Therefore also said the wisdom of God, I will send them prophets and apostles, and some of them they shall slay and persecute: that the blood of all the prophets which was shed from the foundation of the world, may be required of this generation; from the blood of Abel unto the blood of Zacharias, which perished between the altar and the temple; verily I say unto you, it shall be required of this generation. Woe unto you, lawyers! for ye have taken away the key of knowledge: ye entered not in yourselves, and them that were entering in ye hindered.' And as he said these things unto them, the scribes and the Pharisees began to urge him vehemently, and to provoke him to speak of many things: laying wait for him, and seeking to catch something out of his mouth, that they might accuse him." (LUKE 11:37–54)

15

The most unexpected of his qualities is a sense of humor. His worshipers have taken him with deadly seriousness, and will be shocked by the idea that he sometimes jokes. But isn't there some playful exaggeration in the advice that a man should take the beam out of his own eye before he tries to take the mote out of his neighbor's? Or consider the story of the woman taken in adultery, which appears in the John gospel. Read it carefully and use your own sense of humor as you go along:

"Jesus went unto the Mount of Olives. And early in the morning he came again into the temple, and all the people came unto him; and he sat down, and taught them. And the scribes and Pharisees brought unto him a woman taken in adultery; and when they had set her in the midst, they say unto him, 'Master, this woman was taken in adultery, in the very act. Now Moses in the law commanded us, that such should be stoned: but what sayest thou?' This they said, tempting him, that they might have to accuse him. But Jesus stooped down and with his finger wrote on the ground, as though he heard them not. So when they continued asking him, he lifted up himself, and said unto them, 'He that is

without sin among you, let him first cast a stone at her.' And
again he stooped down, and wrote on the ground. And they
which heard it, being convicted by their own conscience,
went out one by one, beginning at the eldest, even unto the
last: and Jesus was left alone, and the woman standing in
the midst. When Jesus had lifted up himself, and saw none
but the woman, he said unto her, 'Woman, where are those
thine accusers? hath no man condemned thee?' She said,
'No man, Lord.' And Jesus said unto her, 'Neither do I condemn thee: go, and sin no more.'"

Consider that little touch of writing on the ground. Who
can imagine the scene without knowing that Jesus had a
smile on his face, while he pretended not to be watching
the woman's accusers as one by one they slunk away abashed.

16

Again, for humor, take the story of the coin of the Roman
Empire. In reading it bear in mind that the coin bore the
image of Caesar, which made it accursed to the Jews, not
merely because Caesar was their conquering lord, but because all images were blasphemy against Yahweh. Bear in
mind also that the episode occurred after Jesus had gone up
to Jerusalem, and was in grave peril from these enemies
whom he was insulting and outraging. He was breaking the
Jewish laws continually, but he was careful to break no
Roman laws. He denounced the priests and the scribes, the
Pharisees and the Sadducees, but he never denounced any
Romans. His Jewish enemies were trying to trap him into
saying something that would make him an enemy of the
Romans, and so enable them to bring a charge against him.
He had referred to Herod Antipas as 'that fox'; but Herod
was in Galilee, the tetrarch of that province. Now Jesus was
in Jerusalem, and if only his enemies could get him to speak
in the same way of the Emperor!

So came the episode which is told in Matthew, Mark and
Luke. "Then went the Pharisees, and took counsel how they
might entangle him in his talk. And they sent out unto him
their disciples with the Herodians, saying, 'Master, we know
that thou art true, and teachest the way of God in truth,
neither carest thou for any man: for thou regardest not the
person of men. Tell us therefore, what thinkest thou? is it
lawful to give tribute unto Caesar, or not?' But Jesus perceived their wickedness, and said, 'Why tempt ye me, ye
hypocrites? Shew me the tribute money.' And they brought

unto him a penny. And he saith unto them, 'Whose is this image and superscription?' They say unto him, 'Caesar's.' Then saith he unto them, 'Render therefore unto Caesar the things which are Caesar's; and unto God the things that are God's.' When they had heard these words, they marvelled, and left him, and went their way." (MATTHEW 22:15-22)

This was a good jest for scribes and Pharisees, but not so good as doctrine to send down through the ages. The ages do not permit their prophets and saints to have a sense of humor; every word they speak is held by zealots to be the Word of God and must be taken literally. This injunction to "render unto Caesar the things which are Caesar's" has been taken as a sanction not only of citizenship but of every form of oppression which has appeared in the world through nineteen centuries. And nothing would have horrified Jesus more; nothing could have been more contrary to his rebel spirit. Jesus himself rendered nothing to Caesar; he had no money, owned no property, and paid no taxes. It was of Caesar he was speaking when he said: "Fear not them which kill the body, but are not able to kill the soul: but rather fear Him which is able to destroy both body and soul in hell."

17

As we follow this story we see the rebel growing more and more conscious of his mission, and more and more sharp in his mood. It is not an easy life to which he calls people. One of his disciples says to him, "Lord, suffer me first to go and bury my father." But Jesus replies, "Follow me; and let the dead bury their dead." There was a certain scribe who came and offered to follow him wherever he would go; and "Jesus saith unto him, 'The foxes have holes, and the birds of the air have nests; but the Son of Man hath not where to lay his head.' "

This Son of Man phrase by which he refers to himself has given trouble to the commentators; some give it one meaning, some another. Jesus uses it eighty-one times in the course of the Gospels. To many devout believers, of course, Son of Man is the same as Son of God; but that is simply because they want it that way. Son of Man means man, of flesh and blood. In the *Book of Daniel* it is used to mean the Messiah, but the Messiah was never God or Son of God to the Jews. As previously stated, the Messiah was sometimes a heavenly being sent to earth by God, and at other times he was a man raised up by God to be the Messiah King and Deliverer of Israel. The Anointed One had oil poured upon his head.

The question as to whether Jesus considered himself a Messiah is one of the most complicated with which we have to deal. It may well be that he did not believe this at the beginning, but came to believe it in the course of his mission. It may be that it was forced upon him by his disciples; it may be that it was a secret he wished to keep from the world. All the sayings in which he pictures himself as sitting at the right hand of God, and his disciples sitting on thrones, we are taking the liberty to set aside; but the question of what he thought about the Messiah was different, and it is quite possible that as the sense of his mission grew upon him, he became certain in his heart that God intended him to fulfill this role of deliverer.

What he talked about, and wanted men to think about, was his Heavenly Father, his loving Father, his Father of justice and mercy. He did not want to be known as a miracle worker, or to exalt himself above other men. What he wanted was to call sinners to repentance, and save their souls before the day of judgment which was expected within a very short time. "Verily I say unto you, this generation shall not pass, till all these things be fulfilled." (MATTHEW 24:34) But he could not tell the day; he said: "But of that day and hour knoweth no man, no, not the angels of heaven, but my Father only." And lest anyone think that in calling God his Father he was proclaiming himself the Son, let it be made clear that he called God *your* Father, too. He said it eighteen times in the New Testament: "Your Heavenly Father knoweth," and so on. He meant that we were all sons of God, and he was one of them. In that sense, we can all be Christians, or at least try to be good enough to deserve the name.

18

We have now witnessed some of the miracles of Jesus, and have heard the crucial portions of his teachings. How much success has he had? By his own standards, not much. To be sure he can gather a crowd any time he wishes, but he does not seem to care for this. He has sent his disciples in pairs to travel over Galilee to make converts, and has given them power "to cast out demons, and to tread on serpents." They have come back reporting some success; but that evidently is not what he wants either. He had sent seventy, two at a time, "before his face into every city and place, whither he himself would come." He had told them that "the harvest is great, but the laborers are few," and that they were to "pray to the Lord of the harvest, that He will send forth laborers into His harvest." They went, and came back and reported with joy saying, "Lord, even the devils are subject unto us through thy name."

But even so, he wasn't satisfied. What was it that he wanted? Evidently not the casting out of devils and the healing of diseases; not anything happening to individuals. He wanted to see some great national change. He wanted to see the chosen people abandon their sinful ways, and repent, and return to the pure worship of their God. He wanted God Himself to do something about this; to intervene and make the world a less terrible place for His servants and true believers to dwell in. He had been certain that God meant to do this, and that the time was short; but by now the time was growing long, and God had not yet done it. Could it be that He had changed His mind? Or had Jesus misread Him? Or was there something displeasing to God in what Jesus was doing?

19

The four Gospels are confused as to the length of the period of Jesus' mission. Learned scholars have studied the records word by word, and their estimates vary from one year and three months to three years. But whatever the period of time, it was too long for the missionary. He decided to go up to Jerusalem and thus force the issue. This was a drastic move, one which might bring his mission into peril. Galilee was a remote land, the place of the 'am ha-aretz, and the Romans didn't pay much attention to what went on there; crowds might assemble, and scatter again, and so long as they broke no law and did no damage, the authorities would not bother. But with Jerusalem it was different; Jerusalem was the center of everything, the capital and site of the Temple. The scribes and Pharisees of Galilee were few, and comparatively unknown, but those in Jerusalem were many, and were the important ones, the haughty. If Jesus went there and said the things which he had been saying in Galilee, there would certainly be an uproar; he must know it, and be planning a challenge.

Why did he do it? This question has been troubling scholarship for a long time. Of course, it does not trouble devout believers; they know it all from revelation. The serpent tempted

Eve, and she disobeyed God's command and ate the apple. That was the Fall of Man, which meant that the human race was condemned to sin and torment, and God had to send His Only Begotten Son down to earth to shed his blood as a sacrifice for the redemption of all the sins of the human race, and to save mankind, or at any rate that portion of mankind which believed in Him and the ritual He had established in His holy Church. All that is perfectly clear; the churches have it worked out to the last detail, duly certified, and you have only to believe, and repent, and you will be saved.

For people who find all that impossible to believe, the problem is not so simple. Those who take Jesus as a man groping for truth and righteousness have to study the confused evidence, the conflicting words, and try to work out a psychological problem. What had happened to Jesus? What did he believe at that moment, and why did he decide upon this sudden challenge to his enemies? I have not attempted to count the number of books that have been published on these questions, but Albert Schweitzer in his "Quest of the Historical Jesus" quotes or refers to three hundred and seven, and there must have been many thousands of articles reviewing these conflicting books and discussing their arguments.

Had Jesus begun to doubt the validity of his mission, or perhaps the effectiveness of its method? Had he become desperate? Had he begun to doubt the immediate prospect of the ending of the world and the coming of God in clouds of glory? Or had he decided to try to force the issue? There are words of his which the scholars describe as 'difficult.' They are in *Luke 11:12.* "And from the days of John the Baptist until now the Kingdom of Heaven suffereth violence, and the violent take it by force." Just what does that mean? Who were the violent, and how were they trying to take Heaven by force, and were they really succeeding? Could you really "take" Heaven, meaning God, and what was the process?

We must try to understand just what the Jewish people meant when they called themselves a 'chosen people,' and God their Father. Once more we refer to the relationship of earthly fathers to their children. Fathers are stern with their children for the children's own good, but they love their children and sometimes can be persuaded to indulge them—if only the children beg and plead enough! If only they do what their father wants for a while, so that his love for them will be increased, he in turn will oblige them. Begging and pleading with your Heavenly Father is prayer, and Jesus never had a moment's doubt concerning the effectiveness of prayer. When he prayed he knew that he was in direct communication with his Heavenly Father, that his Heavenly Father knew every word that he spoke, and even every word that he thought—for there can be such a thing as silent prayer. To labor is to pray, to meditate is to pray, and to think hard about God and try to understand Him and His ways—that also is to pray. When Jesus went out into the desert alone and lifted his hands to God, the convictions which came to his soul were God's answers. He certainly must have been convinced that it was God who was telling him to go up to Jerusalem, and what to do there.

There is an ultimate formula for prayer, "Thy will not mine be done." It is one of the hardest things in the world for man or woman to accept. Whoever we are, and especially if we are propagandists and preachers, we want to tell God about *our* way. We want to find some trick, perhaps by delicate hinting, to let Him know what He really ought to do, and what He really ought to tell the world. In my childhood when I went to church I heard many a preacher doing that very thing, and today, when I turn on the radio and twist the dial, I come upon some shouting evangelist announcing, "O Lord, Thou knowest." He continues telling the Lord whatever he wants the Lord to know, or what he wants the world to believe that the Lord knows. It sounds to me very much like taking the name of the Lord in vain, but it goes on all the time.

20

"Behold, we go up to Jerusalem," Jesus said to his disciples, and proceeded to tell them exactly what was going to happen to them there. He had to know it all in advance, because he was God, and it was all put into the record in order that mankind should know that he was God, and that he had known in advance what was going to happen to him. To me that takes all the life out of the story. If he was in fact God, he could have thought of a thousand better ways to reform and change mankind than to come down to earth disguised as a man and be crucified. It seems to me that it was rather hard on the poor Jews and Romans, who didn't know that he was God, but thought him a disturber of the peace and a false leader of the people. It seems to me it was all the harder because both God and Jesus must have known that the scheme wasn't going to work, but on the contrary would promote religious wars in which millions of human beings would be slaughtered. Surely an infinite and omnipotent and omniscient God could have found better ways to let the world know what He wanted! Even I, with my limited mind, could have suggested to Him how to manage it. (My will not thine be done!)

Just what was Jesus hoping to accomplish in Jerusalem? Was he trying to reform the people there, and make them worthy of the coming of God? Had he decided that Galilee was not enough, but that Judea also must repent and come back to the true worship? Or was he expecting to bring about another exodus, to lead the people out into the desert to live like the Rechabites with John the Baptist? There are some learned scholars who believe that was the case; he hoped thereby to break the will of the Romans, as Moses, with the help of God, had broken the will of the Egyptians. Did he think that he, the messenger of God, the preacher of the new-old righteousness, could by his petitions persuade God to work another series of miracles such as he had done in the days of Moses?

Remember, two thousand years earlier God had come down and talked with Moses again and again. Had He talked with Jesus? Had Jesus now made up his mind that he was the Messiah, and the one destined to bring the evils of the time to a head; to break the power of the wicked men, both Jews and Romans, who were holding the people in servitude? "Whose fan is in his hand," John the Baptist had preached, "and He will thoroughly purge His floor, and gather His wheat into the garners: but He will burn up the chaff with unquenchable fire."

There had been much fire in the message of the Baptist, and in that of the prophets which Jesus knew by heart. Malachi, the last of them, was never out of the thoughts of either Jesus or John. Words such as: " 'For, behold, the day cometh, that shall burn as an oven; and all the proud, yea, and all that do wickedly, shall be stubble: and the day that cometh shall burn them up,' saith the Lord of hosts, 'that it shall leave them neither root nor branch.' " (MALACHI 4:1) The Baptist was rumored to be Elijah, and Malachi had said: "Behold, I will send you Elijah the prophet before the coming of the great and dreadful day of the Lord." (MALACHI 4:5) Again Malachi had said: " 'Behold, I will send My messenger, and he shall prepare the way before Me: and the Lord, whom ye seek, shall suddenly come to His temple, even the messenger of the covenant, whom ye delight in: 'behold, He shall come,' saith the Lord of Hosts; but who may abide the day of His coming? and who shall stand when He appeareth? for He is like a refiner's fire." (MALACHI 3:1-2)

These terrible warnings had been issued four hundred years ago, but they had had no effect; the world was the same wicked place. The prophet had cried in his anguish of soul: "Have we not all one Father? hath not one God created us? why do we deal treacherously every man against his brother, by profaning the covenant of our fathers?" (MALACHI 2:10) And then again: "And now we call the proud happy; yea, they that work wickedness are set up; yea, they that tempt God are even delivered." (MALACHI 3:15)

21

So it had been for ages. They that worked wickedness were still set up, and they that tempted God were still delivered. We cannot understand the mood of Jesus unless we read the history of that time and learn something about its horrible cruelties. After the putting down of the Athronga revolt, Herod's son and successor had crucified two thousand men. During the lifetime of Jesus and his generation there had been no year without revolts and wholesale killings. The Jewish land was in ruins, and the Jewish soul in torment. As Paul wrote, a few years later: "For we know that the whole creation groaneth and travaileth in pain together until now." (ROMANS 8:22) So prevalent was the practice of spying and betraying, there was a saying in the Talmud that men "feared to speak, lest the very fowls of the air should carry the words they had spoken."

The hope of Jesus lay in bringing matters to a head. If his Heavenly Father saw him suffering He would surely intervene and save him. There are many scholars who think that Jesus had become convinced that he was the Messiah; that the pressure upon him by his followers had forced this idea upon him. But the idea of a martyr Messiah was foreign to the Jews, and would have been wholly incomprehensible to them. The Messiah was to come in glory, with the authority of the Lord to end the present evils; or the Messiah was a Jewish leader raised up and endowed with power to perform this service. The idea of a Messiah who could fail, who would

be a sacrifice—no Jew could understand it, and surely no
disciple of Jesus did understand it.

However, the idea of blood sacrifice had come down to the
Jews from earliest time, and was ingrained in their very being. There are in Isaiah chapters which have caused much
speculation, the so-called "Suffering Servant" passages. It is
certain that Jesus must have known these; he probably knew
them by heart, and may have decided that he would be that
Suffering Servant, and assume that prophecy for his fate. Said
Isaiah:

"Who hath believed our report? and to whom is the arm
of the Lord revealed?

"For he shall grow up before him as a tender plant, and as
a root out of a dry ground: he hath no form nor comeliness;
and when we shall see him, there is no beauty that we should
desire him.

"He is despised and rejected of men; a man of sorrows, and
acquainted with grief: and we hid as it were our faces from
him; he was despised, and we esteemed him not.

"Surely he hath borne our griefs, and carried our sorrows:
yet we did esteem him stricken, smitten of God, and afflicted.

"But he was wounded for our transgressions, he was
bruised for our iniquities: the chastisement of our peace was
upon him; and with his stripes we are healed.

"All we like sheep have gone astray; we have turned every
one to his own way; and the Lord hath laid on him the
iniquity of us all.

"He was oppressed, and he was afflicted, yet he opened
not his mouth: he is brought as a lamb to the slaughter, and
as a sheep before her shearers is dumb, so he openeth not his
mouth.

"He was taken from prison and from judgment: and who
shall declare his generation? for he was cut off out of the
land of the living: for the transgression of my people was he
stricken.

"And he made his grave with the wicked, and with the rich
in his death; because he had done no violence, neither was
any deceit in his mouth.

"Yet it pleased the Lord to bruise him; He hath put him
to grief: when Thou shalt make his soul an offering for sin,
he shall see his seed, he shall prolong his days, and the
pleasure of the Lord shall prosper in his hand.

"He shall see of the travail of his soul, and shall be satis-

fied: by his knowledge shall My righteous servant justify
many; for he shall bear their iniquities.

"Therefore will I divide him a portion with the great, and
he shall divide the spoil with the strong; because he hath
poured out his soul unto death: and he was numbered with
the transgressors; and he bare the sin of many, and made in-
tercession for the transgressors." (ISAIAH 53:1–12)

22

The writer, carrying out his duty to this book, has studied
the large and heavy volumes of learned men who have dealt
with the life of Jesus. He finds that they differ among themselves, and the only thing he can say is that he does not
know what was in the mind of Jesus when he said, "Behold,
we go up to Jerusalem." From the writer's own experience of
a half-century as would-be social reformer, he knows that
it is possible for such a man to have many different states
of mind and mood; to be confident, even exultant, and then
again to be besieged by doubts; to be filled with loving-
kindness and again with bitterness and anger; to have friends
and trust them, and then see them betray their cause; to see
them humble and grateful and then see them swell up like
toads, filled with wind and the glory of applause. Goethe in
one of his best-known poems describes the lover as "rejoicing
to heaven, troubled to death"; and that can apply to the lover
of mankind exactly as to the lover of a woman.

Jesus may have changed his mind more than once in his
mission. Many a man has preached idealism, and discovered
that it did not work in practice; many a man has gone out in
the world full of the noblest imaginings and discovered that
he was making himself a victim of rascals and cheats. In the
Sermon on the Mount Jesus said: "And if any man will sue
thee at the law, and take away thy coat, let him have thy
cloke also." (MATTHEW 5:40) And then in the very same
discourse he said: "Give not that which is holy unto the dogs,
neither cast ye your pearls before swine, lest they trample
them under their feet, and turn again and rend you." (MAT-
THEW 7:6) These two injunctions do not seem exactly consistent, and it is permitted us to believe that they were said
at different times in the life of the preacher. They were the
Logia of Jesus, sayings that were circulated widely, and a
century later were gathered and made into a few speeches.

This problem brings to mind the case of Socrates, as told
in Plato's Apology. Socrates was condemned on the charge

of having corrupted the youth of Athens by teaching that the gods did not exist. His friends wished to arrange his escape from prison, but he chose to stay and drink the hemlock. Why? He believed that his death would condemn the law; that out of the event would come a new birth of intellectual honesty. That was four hundred years before Jesus, and it is unlikely that Jesus ever heard the story; but the impulse to hold truth more important than life lies in the heart of all great souls.

Among the many parables which Jesus taught to his disciples was that of the mustard seed; and they, as usual, failed to understand it:

"So is the kingdom of God, as if a man should cast seed into the ground; and should sleep, and rise night and day, and the seed should spring and grow up, he knoweth not how. For the earth bringeth forth fruit of herself; first the blade, then the ear, after that the full corn in the ear. But when the fruit is brought forth, immediately he putteth in the sickle, because the harvest is come. Whereunto shall we liken the kingdom of God? or with what comparison shall we compare it? It is like a grain of mustard seed, which, when it is sown in the earth, is less than all the seeds that be in the earth: but when it is sown, it groweth up, and becometh greater than all herbs, and shooteth out great branches; so that the fowls of the air may lodge under the shadow of it." (MARK 4:26–32)

23

This time the prophet did not travel to Jerusalem by way of the desert. This time he was a known man with many followers, and admirers who were honored to receive him as a guest. His disciples traveled with him, and it must have been quite a cortège; there were women who went along. The story tells that they went by way of Jericho, and that there Jesus restored the sight of a blind man; then they came to the Mount of Olives, which lies just east of Jerusalem, and he told two of his disciples to go to a certain village, and there they would find an ass with a colt, and they were to loose the ass and bring her and her colt to Jesus. The people who were standing nearby asked what the taking of the ass meant, and when they learned that it was for Jesus, they let it go. The story or tradition was included, so that Jesus would be shown entering Jerusalem as the Messiah, according to the prophecy of *Zechariah 9:9*.

To Jesus the people cried, "Hosanna," a Jewish form of

greeting meaning, "Save, I beseech you." They cried: "Blessed is he that cometh in the name of the Lord!"—a quotation from the Psalms. If Jesus did make his entrance in this public and ostentatious way, it must have been a deliberate challenge to his enemies, an invitation to a fight to the death either of his body or of their theocratic power. More than that, he challenged their economic power, for he went directly to the Temple, and there dealt with the moneychangers who had shocked him in his childhood, and whom he had never ceased to resent. This is the story:

"And Jesus went into the Temple, and began to cast out them that sold and bought in the Temple, and overthrew the tables of the moneychangers, and the seats of them that sold doves; and would not suffer that any man should carry any vessel through the Temple. And he taught, saying unto them, 'Is it not written, My house shall be called of all nations the house of prayer? but ye have made it a den of thieves.'" (MARK 11:15–17)

The Fourth Gospel tells the story in greater detail. It says that "Jesus found in the Temple those that sold oxen and sheep and doves, and the changers of money sitting: and when he had made a scourge of small cords, he drove them all out of the Temple, and the sheep, and the oxen; and poured out the changers' money, and overthrew the tables." (JOHN 2:14–15)

24

This is a story which has given comfort and satisfaction to the "radicals" down through the ages. In the interest of truth it must be admitted that it does not seem exactly consistent with the pacifist doctrines of the Sermon on the Mount, and certainly it was an invitation to violence on the part of his enemies, who hitherto had been content to oppose him with sly questions. The scribes and Pharisees could hardly take it as anything less than blasphemy, for the moneychangers had been a part of the Temple system for a long time, and it would be hard to see how the Temple could get its income if the people of the towns who came in to worship and bring their tithes had not been able to buy the animals required by the Law. No wonder "the scribes and the chief priests feared him, and sought how they might destroy him."

When he came back to the Temple the next day they asked him, "By what authority doest thou these things? and who gave thee this authority to do these things?" (MARK 11:28)

Once more Jesus showed his finesse by replying with a subtle evasion. He said unto them: " 'I will also ask of you one question, and answer me, and I will tell you by what authority I do these things. The baptism of John, was it from heaven, or of men? answer me.' And they reasoned with themselves, saying, if we shall say, 'from heaven'; he will say, 'Why then did ye not believe him?' But if we shall say, 'Of men'; they feared the people: for all men counted John, that he was a prophet indeed. And they answered and said unto Jesus, 'We cannot tell.' And Jesus answering saith unto them, 'Neither do I tell you by what authority I do these things.' " (MARK 11:29–33)

It was immediately after this that the Pharisees and the Herodians—that is to say, friends of the Romans—tried to 'catch him in his words' by asking if it was lawful to give tribute to Caesar. Then he made his answer, asking them to produce a coin, showing them the image of Caesar, and telling them to "render unto Caesar the things that are Caesar's, and unto God the things that are God's."

25

After that they gave him no peace, for they knew they had to confute him before the people. The Sadducees, who did not believe in the resurrection of the body, sought to trap him by asking about marriages in heaven. Then came a scribe, asking him which was the first commandment. "Jesus answered him, 'the first of all the commandments is, Hear, O Israel; the Lord our God is one Lord: and thou shalt love the Lord thy God with all thy heart, and with all thy soul, and with all thy mind, and with all thy strength: this is the first commandment. And the second is like, namely this, thou shalt love thy neighbor as thyself. There is none other commandment greater than these.' " (MARK 12:29–31) This scribe was a man of open mind, and he said: " 'Well, Master, thou hast said the truth: for there is one God; and there is none other but He: and to love Him with all the heart, and with all the understanding, and with all the soul, and with all the strength, and to love his neighbor as himself, is more than all whole burnt offerings and sacrifices.' And when Jesus saw that he answered discreetly, he said unto him, 'Thou art not far from the kingdom of God.' And no man after that durst ask him any question." (MARK 12:32–34)

Not all the scribes were like that, as Jesus had known from his childhood. But the common people heard him gladly, when he said, " 'Beware of the scribes, which love to go in long clothing, and love salutations in the marketplaces, and the chief seats in the synagogues, and the uppermost rooms at feasts: which devour widows' houses, and for a pretence make long prayers: these shall receive greater damnation.' " (MARK 12:38–40)

It was there that he gave the friends of the poor and lowly another comment which they might quote through the rest of time. That is the story of the widow's mite. "And Jesus sat over against the treasury, and beheld how the people cast money into the treasury: and many that were rich cast in much; and there came a certain poor widow, and she threw in two mites, which make a farthing. And he called unto him his disciples, and saith unto them, 'Verily I say unto you, that this poor widow hath cast more in, than all they which have cast into the treasury: for all they did cast in of their abundance; but she of her want did cast in all that she had, even all her living.' " (MARK 12:41–44)

All these stories are priceless; but as we read them we have to keep a watchful eye for possible interpolators. In the very next two verses occurs the following: "And as he went out of the temple, one of his disciples saith unto him, 'Master, see what manner of stones and what buildings are here!' And Jesus answering said unto him, 'Seest thou these great buildings? there shall not be left one stone upon another, that shall not be thrown down.' " (MARK 13:1–2)

We have to bear in mind the fact that it was only some forty or fifty years after this episode that an uprising of the Jewish rebels caused the Romans to destroy not merely the Temple but the whole city of Jerusalem, and to run a plow over it. That was before the Gospels had been written, and while they were taking shape as traditions. How easy for some friend of the crucified prophet to put in a remark like that, as proof to all the world that Jesus indeed had been God, knowing all the future, not merely of Jerusalem but of mankind! Of course anyone is free to believe that he said it; I am only saying that it looks like an interpolation to me.

26

Four of the disciples waited until they had Jesus alone. There, "as he sat upon the Mount of Olives over against the Temple" they asked him "privately," "Tell us, when shall these things be? and what shall be the sign when all these things shall be filled?" (MARK 13:4) He answered with a long discourse, something which is rare in the Mark text. This discourse is highly important, as showing his purposes and point of view at the close of his life. It is strictly what the theologians called eschatological, which means having to do with the end of things. I give here enough to convince you that Jesus did believe the end of the world to be close at hand, and that it was the intention of his Heavenly Father either to save him from death, or else to let the world perish —which would amount to the same thing. I take it to be authentic, except for two verses, in which he declares that they shall see the Son of Man coming in the clouds. The rest of the discourse runs: "But when ye shall see the abomination of desolation, spoken of by Daniel the prophet, standing where it ought not, (let him that readeth understand,) then let them that be in Judea flee to the mountains: and let him that is on the house top not go down into the house, neither enter therein, to take anything out of his house: and let him that is in the field not turn back again for to take up his garments. But woe to them that are with child, and to them that give suck in those days! And pray ye that your flight be not in the winter. For in those days shall be affliction, such as was not from the beginning of the creation which God created unto this time, neither shall be. And except that the Lord had shortened those days, no flesh should be saved: but for the elect's sake, whom he hath chosen, he hath shortened the days. And then if any man shall say to you, Lo, here is Christ; or, lo, he is there; believe him not: for false Christs and false prophets shall rise, and shall shew signs and wonders, to seduce, if it were possible, even the elect.

"But take ye heed: behold, I have foretold you all things. But in those days, after that tribulation, the sun shall be darkened, and the moon shall not give her light, and the stars of heaven shall fall, and the powers that are in heaven shall be shaken. And then shall they see the Son of Man coming in the clouds with great power and glory. And then shall he send his angels, and shall gather together his elect from the four winds, from the uttermost part of the earth to the uttermost part of heaven. Now learn a parable of the fig tree; when her branch is yet tender, and putteth forth leaves, ye know that summer is near: so ye in like manner, when ye shall see these things come to pass, know that it is nigh, even at the doors. Verily I say unto you, that this generation shall not pass, till all these things be done; heaven and earth shall pass away: but my words shall not pass away. But of that day and that hour knoweth no man, no, not the angels which are in heaven, neither the Son, but the Father. Take ye heed, watch and pray; for ye know not when the time is." (MARK 13:14–33)

The crucial sentence here, of course, is "That this generation shall not pass, till all these things be done." You can see that Jesus, holding such beliefs, didn't have to worry about what might happen to one man. If his enemies killed him, they would bury him, and he had learned from the prophet Ezekiel what would happen then. "Thus saith the Lord God unto these bones; 'Behold, I will cause breath to enter you, and ye shall live: and I will lay sinews upon you, and will bring up flesh upon you, and cover you with skin, and put breath in you, and ye shall live; and ye shall know that I am the Lord.'" (EZEKIEL 37:5–6) In view of this promise, where could there be any sting in death?

27

The story according to Mark continues: "After two days was the feast of the Passover, and of unleavened bread: and the chief priests and the scribes sought how they might take him by craft, and put him to death. But they said, 'Not on the feast day, lest there be an uproar of the people.'" Then the account tells how Judas Iscariot, one of the chosen apostles, went unto the chief priests to betray Jesus unto them. "And when they heard it, they were glad, and promised to give him money. And he sought how he might conveniently betray him."

The story from then on is full of wonders; Jesus knows everything that is going to happen, and tells about it in advance. There is no need to repeat my point of view, that all this is wisdom after the event. If the reader can believe otherwise, let him do so. From now on I tell the story as Mark tells it, and leave it for the reader to pick and choose, or take it all, according to his own convictions.

"And the first day of unleavened bread, when they killed the Passover, his disciples said unto him, 'Where wilt thou that we go and prepare that thou mayest eat the Passover?' And he sendeth forth two of his disciples, and saith unto them, 'Go ye into the city, and there shall meet you a man bearing a pitcher of water: follow him. And wheresoever he shall go in, say ye to the goodman of the house, The Master saith, *Where is the guestchamber, where I shall eat the Pass-*

over with my disciples? And he will shew you a large upper room furnished and prepared: there make ready for us.' And his disciples went forth, and came into the city, and found as he had said unto them: and they made ready the Passover. And in the evening he cometh with the twelve.

"And as they sat and did eat, Jesus said, 'Verily I say unto you, One of you which eateth with me shall betray me.' And they began to be sorrowful, and to say unto him one by one, 'Is it I?' and another said, 'Is it I?' and he answered and said unto them, 'It is one of the twelve, that dippeth with me in the dish. The Son of Man indeed goeth, as it is written of him: but woe to that man by whom the Son of Man is betrayed! good were it for that man if he had never been born.' And as they did eat, Jesus took bread, and blessed, and brake it, and gave to them, and said, 'Take, eat: this is my body.' And he took the cup, and when he had given thanks, he gave it to them: and they all drank it. And he said unto them, 'This is my blood of the New Testament, which is shed for many. Verily I say unto you, I will drink no more of the fruit of the vine, until that day that I drink it new in the kingdom of God.' And when they had sung an hymn, they went out into the Mount of Olives.

"And Jesus saith unto them, 'All ye shall be offended because of me this night: for it is written, I will smite the shepherd, and the sheep shall be scattered. But after that I am risen, I will go before you into Galilee.' But Peter said unto him, 'Although all shall be offended, yet will not I.' And Jesus saith unto him, 'Verily I say unto thee, That this day, even in this night, before the cock crow twice, thou shalt deny me thrice.' But he spake the more vehemently, 'If I should die with thee, I will not deny thee in any wise.' Likewise also said they all. And they came to a place which was named Gethsemane: and he saith to his disciples, 'Sit ye here, while I shall pray,' and he taketh with him Peter and James and John, and began to be sore amazed, and to be very heavy; and he saith unto them, 'My soul is exceeding sorrowful unto death: tarry ye here, and watch.' And he went forward a little, and fell on the ground, and prayed that, if it were possible, the hour might pass from him. And he said, 'Abba, Father, all things are possible unto thee; take away this cup from me: nevertheless not what I will, but what thou wilt.' "

We permit ourselves here to stop and pray with Jesus, or at any rate to meditate upon his prayer. You perceive that those who tell the story cannot make up their mind whether Jesus is God or whether he is man. Truly it is a difficult problem, once you admit such a thing as the possibility that God may take on the form of a man and come down to earth. When he becomes man, is He man or is He still God? And how can He be betrayed, when He knows He is going to be betrayed? The legend never answers clearly, for basically it is an absurdity and there can be no answer, nor even any rational thought on such a subject.

If Jesus is God, He knows everything in advance. But in that case the procedure means nothing to Him; He is like an actor going through a role, and it must have been a rather tedious role to Omniscience. Is He doing it for the entertainment of children? If so, why not encourage the children to grow up mentally and face the truth? On the other hand, if he is a man and has the mind of a man, then he no longer knows the truth, he no longer possesses the comfort of omniscience. The legend requires that we shall believe both these things at the same time; but manifestly, a man cannot know something and at the same time not know it; he cannot know everything and at the same time grope half-blindly as we human beings are doing all through our lives.

I am convinced he was a man, and that he did not know what was going to happen to him; but he knew that he was in danger, he knew that he had come up here to Jerusalem to challenge the powerful ones of the earth who both hated and feared him. He had come because a voice in his soul which he took to be God told him to come. We all have that voice in our souls, and whether we call it God or whether we call it conscience makes little difference. It is there, and we obey it from inner compulsion, because it is our nature to hear that "still small voice" and to be impelled by it, even as Elijah was impelled when he heard it long ago.

28

Jesus was going ahead to face his enemies and take whatever came to him; but he shrank from it. There is a Civil War story of a sensitive young Southerner going into battle; one of his comrades, seeing the paleness of his face, remarks, "You are scared." The answer is, "Yes, I am scared, and if you were half as scared as I am, you would run away." It is told as a joke, and psychologists know that men joke in time of trouble because they cannot stand it otherwise. Besides the instinct of conscience there is another instinct deeply planted in the human soul, that of survival. Jesus did not want to die, he wanted to live and preach repentance and the forgiveness of sins, and see men respond to his words, and see the coming of peace and happiness on earth. Therefore, he prayed that this cup might pass from him and that he would not have to drink it. So he prayed; but he added, "Nevertheless not what I will, but what thou wilt."

As we have said, this is the hardest of all prayers for a human being to utter. We are not put on this earth to submit, but to struggle and learn and grow. We have our egos and we set a value upon them, and try as we will in our prayers, we cannot help making suggestions to God. We cannot help thinking deep in our souls that surely He can be made to understand what we want and let us have it. But there may come a time when we are helpless, chained and bound, and we can do nothing but submit. The hardest trial of all is when the chains are of our own making—those of conscience. "When duty whispers low, thou must!"

So it was with the young soldier going into battle, and so it was with Jesus going up to Jerusalem. He hadn't wanted to come. He had been afraid of Jerusalem ever since his boyhood, when he came to it so full of hope and reverence, and had made the discovery of its wickedness and corruption. Ever since then he had had it in his thoughts; he had prayed, and this very day he had wept over it with bitter tears. "O Jerusalem, Jerusalem, thou that killest the prophets, and stonest them which are sent unto thee, how often would I have gathered thy children together, even as a hen gathereth her chickens under her wings, and ye would not." (MATTHEW 23:37)

Always in his mind must have been the doubt whether God meant for him to die or meant to rescue him. Maybe he was the Messiah; maybe God had chosen him, as so often in his desert prayers he had imagined; maybe God would come in clouds of glory and bring this whole chain of sin and cruelty to an end. Then his enemies would see that he had been right and that God was on the side of mercy and love. Maybe all that was needed to bring the answer to this prayer was more prayer, harder prayer, the prayer of several righteous men united. Had not the Lord once promised Abraham that He would spare the city of Sodom if Abraham could find ten righteous men in it? Had not Jesus in his Sermon on the Mount told his disciples that if two or three were gathered together in his name, he would be there in the midst of them? But these poor apostles were tired, and could not keep awake; the spirit was willing but the flesh was weak.

As Luke tells the story, an angel came unto him from heaven, strengthening him. I suppose this is a way of symbolizing the fact that in his prayers he found courage. Luke tells us that he prayed so hard that "his sweat was as it were great drops of blood falling down to the ground." The same is supposed to have happened since then, with praying saints; and maybe it did, for the power of suggestion is greater than any limits we can set with our present knowledge.

29

Just before this scene in the Garden of Gethsemane Luke has put in a peculiar detail, one which has puzzled all commentators. Jesus is giving instructions to his apostles, "and they said, 'Lord, behold here are two swords.' And he said unto them, 'It is enough.'"

What does this mean? Has the preacher of the Beatitudes, "Blessed are the meek," and so on, come to believe in violence? Or is he thinking, as some of the churchly scholars have suggested, that his disciples should protect themselves? Certainly it seems a strange decision to be taken by a Son of God, who has come down from heaven in order to die to save mankind. Perhaps some enemy of Jesus inserted this into the story, and pious revisers have failed to perceive its significance.

Anyhow, this is what happened. "And immediately, while he yet spake, cometh Judas, one of the twelve, and with him a great multitude with swords and staves, from the chief priests and the scribes and the elders. And he that betrayed him had given them a token, saying, 'Whomsoever I shall kiss, that same is he; take him, and lead him away safely.' And as soon as he was come, he goeth straightway to him, and saith, 'Master, master'; and kissed him. And they laid their hands on him, and took him. And one of them that stood by drew a sword, and smote a servant of the high priest, and cut off his ear." (MARK 14:43–47)

Luke adds that Jesus touched the man's ear and healed him. Jesus answered and said unto them, 'Are ye come out, as against a thief, with swords and with staves to take me? I was daily with you in the Temple teaching, and ye took me not: but the scriptures must be fulfilled.' And they all forsook him, and fled." (MARK 14:48–50)

30

The Jews had no power to punish this disturber with death, but they could condemn him, and then ask Pilate to confirm the verdict; and this they proceeded to do. The story continues:

"And they led Jesus away to the high priest: and with him were assembled all the chief priests and the elders and the scribes. And Peter followed him afar off, even into the palace of the high priest: and he sat with the servants, and warmed himself at the fire. And the chief priests and all the council sought for witness against Jesus to put him to death; and found none. For many bare false witness against him, but their witness agreed not together. And there arose certain, and bare false witness against him, saying, 'We heard him say, "I will destroy this Temple that is made with hands, and within three days I will build another made without hands."' But neither so did their witness agree together. And the high priest stood up in the midst, and asked Jesus, saying, 'Answerest thou nothing? what is it which these witness against thee?' But he held his peace, and answered nothing. Again the high priest asked him, and said unto him, 'Art thou the Christ, the Son of the Blessed?' and Jesus said, 'I am: and ye shall see the Son of Man sitting on the right hand of power, and coming in the clouds of heaven.'

"Then the high priest rent his clothes, and saith, 'What need we any further witnesses? ye have heard the blasphemy: what think ye?' And they all condemned him to be guilty of death. And some began to spit on him, and to cover his face, and to buffet him, and to say unto him, 'Prophesy': and the servants did strike him with the palms of their hands.

"And as Peter was beneath in the palace, there cometh one of the maids of the high priest: and when she saw Peter warming himself, she looked upon him, and said, 'And thou also wast with Jesus of Nazareth.' But he denied, saying, 'I know not, neither understand I what thou sayest.' And he went out into the porch; and the cock crew. And a maid saw him again, and began to say to them that stood by, 'This is one of them.' And he denied it again. And a little after, they that stood by said again to Peter, 'Surely thou art one of them: for thou art a Galilean, and thy speech agreeth thereto.' But he began to curse and swear, saying, 'I know not this man of whom ye speak.' And the second time the cock crew. And Peter called to mind the word that Jesus said unto him, 'Before the cock crow twice, thou shalt deny me thrice.' And when he thought thereon, he wept." (MARK 14:53–72)

31

There follows one of the great stories of the world, a terrible and tragic story, which will be read and wept over as long as men live on this earth. I will not attempt to add anything to it, nor disturb it with my comments, but give it in the simple and direct words of Mark:

"And straightway in the morning the chief priests held a consultation with the elders and scribes and the whole council, and bound Jesus, and carried him away, and delivered him to Pilate. And Pilate asked him, 'Art thou the King of the Jews?' And he answering said unto him, 'Thou sayest it.' And the chief priests accused him of many things: but he answered nothing. And Pilate asked him again, saying, 'Answerest thou nothing? behold how many things they witness against thee.' But Jesus yet answered nothing; so that Pilate marvelled.

"Now at that feast he released unto them one prisoner, whomsoever they desired. And there was one named Barabbas, which lay bound with them that had made insurrection with him, who had committed murder in the insurrection. And the multitude crying aloud began to desire him to do as he had ever done unto them. But Pilate answered them, saying, 'Will ye that I release unto you the King of the Jews?' For he knew that the chief priests had delivered him for envy. But the chief priests moved the people, that he should rather release Barabbas unto them. And Pilate answered and said again unto them, 'What will ye then that I shall do unto him whom ye call the King of the Jews?' And they cried out again, 'Crucify him.' Then Pilate said unto them, 'Why, what evil hath he done?' And they cried out the more exceedingly, 'Crucify him.' And so Pilate, willing to content the people, released Barabbas unto them, and delivered Jesus, when he had scourged him, to be crucified.

"And the soldiers led him away into the hall, called Praetorium; and they called together the whole band. And they clothed him with purple, and platted a crown of thorns, and put it about his head, and began to salute him, 'Hail, King of the Jews!' And they smote him on the head with a reed, and did spit upon him, and bowing their knees worshipped him. And when they had mocked him, they took off the purple from him, and put his own clothes on him, and led him away to crucify him. And they compel one Simon, a Cyrenian, who passed by, coming out of the country, the father of Alexander and Rufus, to bear his cross. And they bring him unto the place Golgotha, which is, being interpreted, 'the place of a skull.' And they gave him to drink wine mingled with myrrh: but he received it not. And when they had crucified him, they parted his garments, casting lots upon them, what every man should take. And it was the third hour, and they crucified him. And the superscription of his accusation was written over, THE KING OF THE JEWS.

"And with him they crucify two thieves; the one on his right hand, and the other on his left. And the scripture was fulfilled, which saith, 'And he was numbered with the transgressors.' And they that passed by railed on him, wagging their heads, and saying, 'Ah, thou that destroyest the Temple, and buildest it in three days, save thyself, and come down from the cross.' Likewise also the chief priests mocking said among themselves with the scribes, 'He saved others; himself he cannot save. Let Christ the King of Israel descend now from the cross, that we may see and believe.' And they that were crucified with him reviled him. And when the sixth hour was come, there was darkness over the whole land until the ninth hour. And at the ninth hour Jesus cried with a loud voice, saying, '*Eloi, Eloi, lama sabachthani?*' which is, being interpreted, 'My God, my God, why hast thou forsaken me?' And some of them that stood by, when they heard it, said, 'Behold, he calleth Elias.' And one ran and filled a sponge full of vinegar, and put it on a reed, and gave him to drink, saying, 'Let alone; let us see whether Elias will come to take him down.' And Jesus cried with a loud voice, and gave up the ghost. And the veil of the Temple was rent in twain from the top to the bottom. And when the centurion, which stood over against him, saw that he so cried out, and gave up the ghost, he said, 'Truly this man was the Son of God.' " (MARK 15:1–39)

Such is the story of the crucifixion and death of Jesus, called the Christ.

BOOK THREE

SPIRIT

❋ ❋ ❋

1

JESUS was dead: but his spirit lived on, and it is this spirit
we now have to follow through nineteen hundred years of
history which it has helped to make.

The wonders began at once, as you have seen. The more
imaginative Matthew tells us that "The veil of the Temple
was rent in twain from the top to the bottom; and the earth
did quake, and the rocks rent; and the graves were opened;
and many bodies of the saints which slept arose, and came
out of the graves after his resurrection, and went into the
holy city, and appeared unto many."

Learned scholars have searched the astronomical records
of the time in all languages known, in the hope of finding
records of earthquakes and eclipses of the sun that fit in with
this story. They have even tried to set the date of the event
according to an eclipse recorded. To all that it seems sufficient to answer in the words of Jesus himself: "An evil and
adulterous generation seeketh after a sign."

We are preparing to watch the development of a legend.
We must not be contemptuous or flippant about it, but must
understand that human beings have been striving with their
limited faculties to express their sense of reverence for a noble
personality, their grief at his tragic fate, and their gratitude
for his effort to save them from their sins, and from the bitter
consequences of all the sins which men commit upon earth.
But at the same time we have to speak the truth. We must try
to separate what happened from what did not happen. We
must try to separate what Jesus said from what the pious
interpolators have made him say. We must sift out from his
touching story the fabulous things which no man could do,
and which Jesus would have been the first to repudiate. He
has given us the truth in the plainest possible words, of which
I remind you again: "Why callest thou me good? there is none
good but one, that is God." He has forbidden us explicitly to

117

seek after signs and wonders in his life. And he has told us the Law, and the highest Law: "*Thou shalt love the Lord thy God with all thy heart, and with all thy soul, and with all thy mind.* This is the first and great commandment. And the second is like unto it, *Thou shalt love thy neighbour as thyself.* On these two commandments hang all the law and the prophets." (MATTHEW 22:37–40)

In this spirit and to this end we proceed to study what mankind has done to the memory of Jesus the Christ through the centuries since he gave up the ghost on the cross.

2

Here is Mark's story of what happened in the next days:

"There were also women looking on afar off: among whom was Mary Magdalene, and Mary the mother of James the Less and of Joses, and Salome; (who also, when he was in Galilee, followed him, and ministered unto him;) and many other women which came up with him unto Jerusalem. And now when the even was come, because it was the preparation, that is, the day before the Sabbath, Joseph of Arimathaea, an honourable counsellor, which also waited for the kingdom of God, came, and went in boldly unto Pilate, and craved the body of Jesus. And Pilate marvelled if he were already dead: and calling unto him the centurion, he gave the body to Joseph. And he brought fine linen, and took him down, and wrapped him in the linen, and laid him in a sepulchre which was hewn out of a rock, and rolled a stone unto the door of the sepulchre. And Mary Magdalene and Mary the mother of Joses beheld where he was laid." (MARK 15:40–47)

"And when the Sabbath was past, Mary Magdalene, and Mary the mother of James, and Salome, had bought sweet spices, that they might come and anoint him. And very early in the morning the first day of the week, they came unto the sepulchre at the rising of the sun. And they said among themselves, 'Who shall roll us away the stone from the door of the sepulchre?' And when they looked, they saw that the stone was rolled away: for it was very great. And entering into the sepulchre, they saw a young man sitting on the right side, clothed in a long, white garment; and they were affrighted. And he saith unto them, 'Be not affrighted: ye seek Jesus of Nazareth, which was crucified: he is risen: he is not here: behold the place where they laid him. But go your way, tell his disciples and Peter that he goeth before you into Galilee: there shall ye see him, as he said unto you.' And they went out quickly, and fled from the sepulchre; for they trembled and were amazed: neither said they any thing to any man; for they were afraid.

"Now when Jesus was risen early the first day of the week, he appeared first to Mary Magdalene, out of whom he had cast seven devils. And she went and told them that had been with him, as they mourned and wept. And they, when they had heard that he was alive, and had been seen of her, believed not.

"After that he appeared in another form unto two of them, as they walked, and went into the country. And they went and told it unto the residue: neither believed they them. Afterward he appeared unto the eleven as they sat at meat, and upbraided them with their unbelief and hardness of heart, because they believed not them which had seen him after he was risen. And he said unto them, 'Go ye into all the world, and preach the Gospel to every creature. He that believeth and is baptized shall be saved; but he that believeth not shall be damned. And these signs shall follow them that believe; in my name shall they cast out devils; they shall speak with new tongues; they shall take up serpents; and if they drink any deadly thing, it shall not hurt them; they shall lay hands on the sick, and they shall recover.' So then after the Lord had spoken unto them, he was received up into heaven, and sat on the right hand of God. And they went forth, and preached every where, the Lord working with them, and confirming the word with signs following. Amen." (MARK 16:1–20)

3

From the other Gospels we get additional details, some of them contradictory. From Matthew we learn that the angel of the Lord descended from heaven, and came and rolled back the stone from the door and sat upon it. (MATTHEW 28:3–4) Matthew also tells us: "When the chief priests of the city learned what was happening they assembled with the elders and took counsel, then they gave large money unto the soldiers, saying, 'Say ye, His disciples came by night, and stole him away while we slept. And if this come to the governor's ears, we will persuade him, and secure you.' So they took the money and did as they were taught: and this saying is commonly reported among the Jews until this day."

In Luke we find the story of the visit at Emmaus, of which there exists a famous painting by Rembrandt: "Two of the disciples went that same day to a village called Emmaus, which was from Jerusalem about threescore furlongs. And they talked together of all these things which had happened. And it came to pass, that, while they communed together and reasoned, Jesus himself drew near, and went with them. But their eyes were holden that they should not know him."

They did not recognize him until they sat at meat. "He took bread, and blessed it, and brake, and gave to them. And their eyes were opened, and they knew him; and he vanished out of their sight. And they said one to another, 'Did not our heart burn within us, while he talked with us by the way, and while he opened to us the scriptures?' and they rose up the same hour, and returned to Jerusalem, and found the eleven gathered together, and them that were with them, saying, 'The Lord is risen indeed, and hath appeared to Simon.' And they told what things were done in the way, and how he was known of them in breaking of bread. And as they thus spake, Jesus himself stood in the midst of them, and saith unto them, 'Peace be unto you.' But they were terrified and affrighted, and supposed that they had seen a spirit. And he said unto them, 'Why are ye troubled? and why do thoughts arise in your hearts? Behold my hands and my feet, that it is I myself: handle me, and see; for a spirit hath not flesh and bones, as ye see me have.' And when he had thus spoken, he shewed them his hands and his feet. And while they yet believed not for joy, and wondered, he said unto them, 'Have ye here any meat?' and they gave him a piece of a broiled fish, and of an honeycomb. And he took it, and did eat before them." (LUKE 24:30–43)

4

Then he told them about repentance and remission of sins "that should be preached in his name among all nations beginning at Jerusalem. And it came to pass, while he blessed them, he was parted from them, and carried up into heaven. And they worshipped him, and returned to Jerusalem with great joy: and were continually in the Temple, praising and blessing God. Amen." (LUKE 24:51–53)

It is interesting to note that in Luke's version, when the women came to the tomb they found "two men in shining garments," that is, angels. Also it is to be noted that in this version, Jesus denied that he was merely a spirit, and showed them his hands and his feet. This is the only place in which there is indication that the crucified one had nails driven through his feet. Painters of the event all through the centuries have taken up the idea. It seems to indicate that the story of Luke was written by someone who knew nothing about this crucifixion or any other; for the Romans had never heard of driving nails through the feet. The victim was nailed through the wrists, and he hung by the wrists. (If the nails had been driven through the hands, the weight of the body would have pulled the hands loose.)

In the narrative of John, Jesus shows his hands and his side which had been wounded by the spear. He makes an elaborate reappearance in this gospel, and even shows Peter how to catch fish—"great fishes, an hundred and fifty and three, and yet there was not a net broken." The story concludes with the following statement: "And there are also many other things which Jesus did, the which, if they should be written every one, I suppose that even the world itself could not contain the books that should be written. Amen." (JOHN 21:25)

So now we have a real problem in miracles; a ghost which is not a ghost but is a real body and eats food. The rationalists of Bible criticism take up the idea of the hostile Jews, that Jesus didn't die on the cross, but was taken down prematurely and spirited out of the tomb by his disciples. The devout, of course, have no difficulty at all; they are quite sure that Jesus was taken physically up into the sky, according to the words of Luke: "And it came to pass, while he blessed them, he was parted from them, and carried up into heaven." (LUKE 24:51) How far he was carried and by what means of transportation is not revealed. We are told in *Acts* that a cloud received him; but we are not told what this cloud was made of or where it took him. It is needless to point out that none of this accords with present-day astronomical knowledge.

5

The reports of the physical reappearance of Jesus of course created tremendous uproar among the Jews of both Jerusalem and Palestine, who had met him and heard him and witnessed his miraculous healings. The centurion who had directed the crucifixion had feared greatly and exclaimed, "Truly this was the Son of God!" Others began saying that, and an excitement started that was to spread all over the world.

What are we going to make of these reappearances of Jesus? I have my own explanation, and state it with sad awareness that it will do no good to either this book or its

author. All my thinking life I have been investigating what
are called psychic phenomena, and I am as certain of their
reality as I am of my own. I do not know what they are, or
how they come to be; I only know that they happen. They
have been happening all through the ages and all over the
world. They are happening today, as you can satisfy yourself
if you choose to take the trouble. I have taken that trouble,
and have witnessed some.

I consider the idea that there was a ghost of Jesus. I never
before heard of a ghost that ate, and it is a little difficult to
imagine what could become of the food. Bear in mind that the
Pharisees had been teaching for a couple of hundred years the
resurrection of the body, and that by now most Jews accepted
the dogma. It was Jews who were bringing into being this new
legend, and so to them it was obvious that the resurrected
Messiah would eat food, and show his wounds, and prove his
physical reality by helping to catch fish in the Lake of Galilee,
something which as a wanderer he had occasionally done.

I have no difficulty in believing that a ghost of Jesus may
have appeared to his followers, and talked with them and told
them whatever he would have told them had he been alive. I
don't think he told them that he was the Son of God, or a
part of God, or anything resembling that. He may have told
them that he was Jesus the Christ, the word Christ meaning
Anointed, the one chosen by God to be the bearer of a new
revelation. This is one of the cases where we have to choose
what seems credible and reject what seems unlikely.

He may have said anything that his disciples believed, or
would have imagined; but that wouldn't include the statement
that he was God, for they were all good Jews, and would have
been shocked by the idea. Such an idea could take root only
when his story and his teachings had begun to spread among
the gentiles; for the gentiles were heathen and idol worshipers,
and it was easy for them to believe that a woman could have
been made pregnant by a god, and borne a son who was a
demigod, or who was part of a Holy Trinity of Gods, or however you choose to phrase the fantasy. The metaphysical
words and the capital letters wouldn't have made a bit of
difference to Jesus; to him it would all have been polytheism
and heathenism.

I do not know what a ghost is. I do not say that it is the
spirit of a dead person; indeed I am rather inclined to guess
that it is not. I try to explain it to myself as some sort of
projection of the subconscious minds of living persons. It

may be a projection of combined subconscious forces, possibly of the mind of the whole universe. I myself have never seen a ghost, but I know persons who have seen them and talked to them. I have been convinced against my will, and solely out of my respect for facts. Some of the wisest men I have known have shared this belief and their testimony is surely apposite to the Jesus story. What happens today could surely happen then.

6

The first such person was the Reverend Minot J. Savage, minister of the Church of the Messiah, Unitarian, in New York. At the age of sixteen, when I was seeking some rational statement of religious belief, I came upon a book by this extremely intelligent and kind gentleman, and went to make his acquaintance. I have never forgotten my consternation as I listened to his story of how he had seen and talked with a ghost. You may find his experiences in his book called *Psychics, Facts and Theories,* then newly published.

In Baltimore, where I was born and spent my childhood, I had been properly taught that the idea of ghosts was nonsense, and that only 'colored folks' believed such things; but now here was a highly educated, liberal-minded, conscientious man, assuring me that he had talked with a ghost. He gave no signs of craziness or fanaticism. This led me to the subject of psychic research; I read a score of books on the subject, including the classical work of F. W. H. Myers, *Human Personality, and Its Survival of Bodily Death.* You may find that in your library, and perhaps also the two-volume work by Edmund Gurney, researcher of the London Society for Psychical Research. The work is entitled *Phantasms of the Living,* and in it you can read seven hundred and three verified cases of apparitions or appearances or manifestations of persons who had just died, or were at the point of dying, or were in serious trouble or fear. The apparitions sometimes appeared to relatives or friends, sometimes to strangers. Often notations had been made at the time, and documents were furnished to the investigator. As a rule the witnesses were educated persons, mostly English. The manifestations appeared sometimes at great distances; for this, apparently, is no bar to the phenomenon.

Some twenty years ago Professor William McDougall came to lecture at the University of California in Los Angeles. He was an Ulsterman who had been for many years head of the

Department of Psychology at Harvard, and was frequently referred as "the dean of American psychology." He came to visit us several times, because of his interest in experiments which my wife and I had conducted, proving the reality of telepathy and clairvoyance. You may read about this in my book, *Mental Radio*, if you are interested; a book to which McDougall wrote a preface. He brought an English colleague named Keatinge, also lecturing at the university, and we learned to know him and his wife well. This quiet and agreeable English lady assured us that she had many times seen ghosts and talked with them. It is, she reported, a strange gift, and she was curious about it and not at all frightened by the experiences. Were we to say that this university professor's wife was mentally or morally unbalanced? She gave no signs of anything of the sort.

Dr. Alexis Carrel made a thorough investigation of these matters, and in *Man the Unknown* he writes: "Telepathic communications occur frequently. In many instances, at the time of death or of great danger, an individual is brought into a certain kind of relation with another. The dying man, or the victim of an accident, even when such accident is not followed by death, appears to a friend in his usual aspect. The phantom generally remains silent. Sometimes he speaks and announces his death."

Telepathy and clairvoyance are common in the Gospel stories; they are common throughout all historic records, and in the literature of modern psychic research. Having witnessed the demonstrations set forth in *Mental Radio*, I have no difficulty in believing the episode told in *John 1:48*, where Jesus had a clairvoyant vision of Nathanael under a figtree, and when Nathanael came he said, "Behold an Israelite indeed, in whom there is no guile!" Or the episode in *Mark 14:15*, where Jesus foresaw the man "bearing a pitcher of water," who would prepare the guest chamber wherein Jesus would eat the Passover with his disciples. In the course of some sixty years study of this subject, I must have met personally several hundred persons who have had such experiences, and many who had them continually, and were accustomed to base their affairs upon them, just as Jesus did. You can hardly mention the subject in any company without someone telling of a case. The latest instance, my friend S. K. Ratcliffe, English journalist, reads the manuscript of this book, and writes:

"Here is something that will interest you for the Miracles

chapter. The one and only churchman who has conquered a huge radio audience here is Canon W. H. Elliott. For eight years he had a weekly audience for a short, late-evening service with a very brief address—untheological, simple, direct. The response was tremendous.

"He has published his reminiscences: *Undiscovered Ends* (Peter Davies). His life is a triumph of will. He can't remember one day of normal good health; for forty years he had a goitre. Nevertheless he worked, and preached, steadily.

"He has a chapter on his experiences of the Unseen. Some of it reads to me like sheer superstition, ludicrous; but his examples of telepathy are remarkable, and undeniable. For example: he was senior curate in a large parish of Leeds. One evening he was resolved to preach although so ill as to be near collapse. A colleague, convinced that he must break down, made out the heads of a sermon during the singing of the psalms in case he (the colleague) should be called upon. Elliott got through surprisingly. His colleague asked him how he had got hold of the colleague's sermon. He showed his heads and a very unusual text which Elliott had used. Another of Elliott's experiences was a nervous knockout in a bookshop, at the moment when his son was killed in a van mishap at Benbury Cross."

7

We are only at the beginning of efforts to understand the human mind. There is apparently a whole universe here, of which we have knowledge akin to what men had of astronomy before the telescope was invented. We talk glibly about the subconscious mind, but I say once more that we don't know what it is and have no idea how it operates. I am producing this book with the help of a tape recording machine. I know how my hand moves the lever, but no scientist can explain how it comes about that the idea of a completed sentence in my mind causes my hand to move to the lever. We say that it is the brain, but how is it that a thought in the brain or anywhere else can cause the movement of a physical object such as a hand? It is like a miracle every time it happens, and the only reason we don't call it a miracle is because it happens thousands of times a day and we take it for granted.

This much we do know. Thought is accompanied by brain waves, which scientists have measured and recorded. Whether the waves cause the thought, or the thoughts cause the waves we cannot say. Is it not reasonable to guess that operations of the subconscious mind also cause, or are caused by, vibratory rates? And who can guess where or how these activities may be spread, and what effect they may have upon others? What more likely than that a man who is dying, or even one who has just died, may originate impulses of some sort which affect the minds of friends? We know that the body disintegrates, but there is left a hard core, the skeleton, which continues to exist for ages. Might there not be a hard core of the mind, or the personality, which has some way of manifesting itself? I cannot say Yes; but can you say No?

Modern physics presents us with a chart of vibratory rates, beginning with radio waves which are measured in miles, and coming down through radio waves, short and ultrashort, microwaves, heat waves, visible light, ultra-violet and X-waves, gamma waves, and secondary cosmic waves so short that it takes a trillion of them to make a millimeter, and with cycles of three trillion billions per second. All these are power, and many of them are still entirely unexplored; what they may be doing to our minds and our bodies we can not even guess. What messages they may be carrying—if only we could read them! It becomes us to be humble and open-minded to every new fact, however unlikely it may at first appear.

I know that in expressing a belief in psychic phenomena, I have repelled many readers, and forfeited respect of some even among my friends. But I am content to join with some of the ablest minds of recent times, including scientists such as Sir William Crookes, Sir Oliver Lodge, and Dr. Alexis Carrel; and psychologists such as Professor William McDougall and Professor William James. The last-named was never quite convinced, but he wrote of the medium Mrs. Piper, that you had either to believe in her spirit controls, or else that she had access to the minds of all persons living.

There was then no such thing as a society for psychical research, and no volumes with thousands of such cases gathering dust on the shelves of libraries. To the people of Jerusalem and Galilee it was a supernatural manifestation; a man whom the Romans had crucified had risen from the dead and ascended into heaven. It was Jesus of Nazareth, son of the carpenter Joseph. A 'good thing' had come out of Nazareth after all! A wonder worker had been born there, a Messiah who had come to redeem mankind and bring the world to an end! They had prayed to God, and He had answered.

Above all things men have feared death, and death is what impresses them—especially when it is a cruel death, a pictur-

esque death, appealing to primitive imaginations. A man hang-
ing with nails through his wrists! A man on a cross high up
in the sky, plainly visible, standing out above everything else!
A grand subject for painters and poets, and a symbol for the
ages!

In the John Gospel we hear Jesus himself saying, "Greater
love hath no man than this, that a man lay down his life for
his friends." And now Jesus himself had done this; he had laid
down his life for mankind. Of course, he had to have something
more than just a life to contribute. Men are dying by thousands every day, and we have no time to think about them.
But this man had had a mind and had expressed it in golden
words. He had had a special power to arouse love and affection
in both men and women. The fishermen had left their nets and
followed him; the women had come in haste to pour ointment
upon his head, to wash his feet, to prepare food for him and
serve it. In spite of his humble dress and appearance, he had
been able to win souls wherever he went.

And now the cruel masters of this world had made him into
a martyr! Someone has to die for a cause if it is to get
started; someone has to die for a truth if it is to be believed.
Had Jesus known this, and had he gone deliberately to his
death? It looks very much as if he had challenged both the
Pharisees and the Romans to put him to death; perhaps
hoping to move the hearts of men, perhaps even to move the
heart of God. Anyhow, he was dead, and he had risen, and
had been taken up to heaven! Wonder of wonders!

8

The rumors spread rapidly over the Jewish land, and as they
spread they grew. There is a little comedy by the Irish play-
wright, Lady Gregory, called "Spreading the News." We see
some trivial incident in an Irish village, something which
starts an excitement, and then we hear the account of it passed
on from one group to the next, constantly being added to until it becomes a tremendous scandal. The story of the life and
death of Jesus underwent a similar fate, but instead of taking
half an hour, as in the one-act play, it took centuries; it went
all over the then-known world, and everywhere it went it was
added to in a different way, to increase its appeal to a particular people—conforming to the beliefs which they already
cherished and were reluctant to give up.

The Jews had the first handling of the story, and of course
the embellishments they supplied were Jewish. They had many

rites and they now made them over for Christian use. Thus
with the ancient practice of baptism, of taking a person into
a river and dipping him to wash his sins away. The Pharisees
had baptized proselytes both male and female. Jesus had been
baptized by John. Now, his disciples started baptizing all
over the place, and baptism became a Christian means of salvation. It must be done in the name of this new Messiah, this
Anointed One, who now dwelt in heaven, and who, if you
gained his favor, would intercede for you there and save your
soul. In course of time the sects were disputing as to whether
the proper way was by total immersion, or by marking a cross
on the forehead with holy water, or by sprinkling the top of
the head; also whether it should be infant baptism or adult,
and so on through controversies that may last so long as
there is a credulous person left on earth.

9

Then there was the Jewish Passover, which Jesus had known
from infancy. When he went up to Jerusalem at Passover
time, he presumably chose that time because there would be a
great many people there, and he could make converts, and
also a conspicuous challenge to the perverters of the Law and
the prophets. He had supper with disciples the night before
his death, but there is no word about his sacrificing and
eating a Paschal lamb. Sitting at supper with his disciples,
and knowing the peril in which he stood, he had eaten bread
and drunk wine with them, and may very well have said
something to the effect that this might be their last meal
together, and that they would remember it. So now the
Jewish disciples took their Passover and devised a ceremony
in which Jesus was made to say, "This is my blood of the New
Testament, which is shed for many for the remission of sins."
(MATTHEW 26:28)

From this has come a procedure called the Eucharist, the
Communion, the Mass; a ceremony of unimaginable solemnity.
Instead of sacrificing a helpless lamb, it is the body of Jesus
which was sacrificed on the cross, it is his blood which was
shed, and by supernatural transformation the bread and wine
become his body and blood, and you reverently eat and drink,
or let the priest do it for you. Billions of words have been
spent in argument, and thousands of tomes have been printed
over the question of just how this metamorphosis takes place.
There is transsubstantiation and there is consubstantiation
and there is a third variety called impanation. The Catholics

hold for what they call the Real Presence; that is, they say that the bread and wine become the actual physical body and blood, even though their appearance remains the same as bread and wine. All devout Catholics have to go once a week and witness this act performed by the priest, and then they know that their souls are safe from hell fire. I don't want to hurt anyone's feelings, and so I content myself with saying that I don't believe Jesus would have had any interest in the procedure.

10

Also, the Jews had rites by which holy succession was determined. Thus the prophet Elijah had cast his mantle upon Elisha to make him the prophet when Elijah was taken up to heaven in a chariot. There was a great deal of anointing of prophets and kings in order to confer divine authority upon them. Now the apostles had to have a ceremony, and it took the form of the laying on of hands. Thus came to be what is called the Apostolic Succession. All Catholics and many Protestant Episcopalians believe that their priests operate by the power conferred upon them in an unbroken line of succession from Simon Peter. They overlook the fact that Peter thrice denied his Lord on the night of his arrest. Someone put into the record a story that Jesus conferred special authority upon this particular apostle during the famous episode in Caesarea Philippi already quoted. Jesus said to Peter: " 'And I say also unto thee, that thou are Peter, and upon this rock I will build my church; and the gates of hell shall not prevail against it.' " (MATTHEW 16:18)

The word Peter, *petros* in Greek, means rock; so Jesus was making a pun. He was saying, "Thou art Rock and upon this rock I will build my church." Then he is made to go on and add, " 'And I will give unto thee the keys of the kingdom of heaven: and whatsoever thou shalt bind on earth shall be bound in heaven: and whatsoever thou shalt loose on earth shall be loosed in heaven.' " (MATTHEW 16:19) Concerning this I can only say that it carries no conviction to me. I feel sure that Jesus had no idea of founding a church; on the contrary he stated over and over that the end of the world was coming before this present generation had passed away. (MAT-THEW 24:34; MARK 13:30–31; LUKE 21:31–32) Also nothing could seem to me more out of order than to imagine Jesus conferring upon one of his apostles the powers which belonged to the Lord God Almighty. Jesus himself would never have dreamed of claiming such powers.

Apparently the "rock" passage was inserted late in the development of the new Church, when its priests desired to establish their authority, and to be in a position to threaten heretics and unbelievers with the torments of hell. Its effect was to put a human intermediary or intercessor between man and God, and thus to put human souls at the mercy of priest-craft. I believe that nothing could have been more abhorrent to Jesus; it was the very basis of his revolt against the church system of his time. "Blessed are the pure in heart," he said, "for they shall see God." Nothing could be more explicit than this. He added, "Blessed are the peacemakers, for they shall be called the children of God." He doesn't say that blessed are those who can get some priest or bishop or archbishop or cardinal or pope to intercede with God for them; he doesn't say blessed are those who pronounce certain magic words; he doesn't say blessed are those who are baptized, or blessed are those who attend Mass, or blessed are those who keep the Sabbath—on the contrary he said that Sabbath was made for man and not man for the Sabbath. He tells you in eleven of the simplest words imaginable, that if you want to see God what you have to do is to be pure in heart. This is something very hard to do, and that is why men proceed to substitute easier things for it.

11

In telling the story of Jesus so far I have tried to leave out negative things and concentrate on the positive; that is, I have chosen the sayings which I think are consistent with his character as I have come to know it. I have omitted most of the things I don't think he said, and the miracles I don't think he performed, and the legends I believe were invented after-wards in order to prove that he was a divinity and had fulfilled all the prophecies of ancient Hebrew poets. But the story of Christianity would not be complete without these things, be-cause the legends were taken up and made into creeds, rituals, and holy traditions. To many people that is Christianity, and it is one of the things that keep Christianity from having the respect of modern educated persons. I am endeavoring to show that these things are excrescences, and that Christianity as it exists today has very little to do with Jesus. But my pur-pose is not negative or destructive. I think that these excres-cences can be cleared away from Christianity, and that the

Church can come back to its glorious exemplar and make itself pure in heart in order that it may see God.

The Jews believed in angels. The word is derived from a Greek word meaning messenger or bearer of tidings. The Pharisees had been at pains to invent a large number of angels having names, and now it was inevitable that Jewish disciples should bring angels into the story of Jesus. Impossible that there could be a new Jewish Messiah, an Anointed One, without plenty of angels to announce and attend him. So in Luke we find a legend about Zacharias, a priest, and how the angel Gabriel, "that stands in the presence of God," was sent to speak with him and tell him that his wife "who was well-stricken in years" was going to bear a child "who shall be filled with the Holy Ghost." Because this priest couldn't believe this message, the angel struck him dumb until such a time as the child should be born. All this in order to make John the Baptist, the forerunner of Jesus, into a magical being.

Then after doing this miracle the angel went to a virgin who lived in Galilee and whose name was Mary, and told her about how she was highly favored. "The Lord is with thee; blessed art thou among women." The angel told her that she had found favor with God. " 'And, behold, thou shalt conceivé in thy womb, and bring forth a son, and shalt call his name JESUS. He shall be great, and shall be called the Son of the Highest: and the Lord God shall give unto him the throne of his father David: and he shall reign over the house of Jacob for ever; and of his kingdom there shall be no end.' Then said Mary unto the angel, 'How shall this be, seeing I know not a man?' and the angel answered and said unto her, 'The Holy Ghost shall come upon thee, and the power of the Highest shall overshadow thee: therefore also that holy thing which shall be born of thee shall be called the Son of God. And, behold, thy cousin Elisabeth, she hath also conceived a son in her old age: and this is the sixth month with her, who was called barren. For with God nothing shall be impossible.' And Mary said, 'Behold the handmaid of the Lord; be it unto me according to thy word.' And the angel departed from her."

Luke is the storyteller who appreciates drama, and puts the human interest into the bare narrative of Mark. He has Mary go to see Elisabeth, and Elisabeth tells how the babe leaped in her womb for joy. Mary recites what is called the Magnificat; a regular Hebrew psalm, as good as the best. It includes the statement, "He hath shewed strength with his arm; He hath scattered the proud in the imagination of their

hearts. He hath put down the mighty from their seats, and
exalted them of low degree. He hath filled the hungry with
good things; and the rich. He has sent empty away."
(LUKE 1:51–53) This was embarrassing to the mighty ones of
future time who were operating in the name of Mary's son,
and it may be among the reasons why throughout the ages
the Catholic Church has carried on its services in a language
its congregations cannot understand. As a poet of recent times
has said:

> 'Tis well that such seditious songs are sung,
> Only in church and in the Latin tongue.

John the Baptist was born, and then it was the turn of his
father, Zacharias, to be filled with the Holy Ghost, and to
chant a psalm in which he listed most of the wonders which
were coming into the world through his son. "And thou, child,
shalt be called the prophet of the highest; for thou shalt go
before the face of the Lord to prepare His ways; to give
knowledge of salvation unto His people by the remission of
their sins, through the tender mercy of our God; whereby the
dayspring from high hath visited us." (LUKE 1:76–78)

12

There were no Jewish novels or novelists in those days; but
their poets made songs about the things that had happened
long ago, and endowed the holy men of that time with foreknowledge. So, of course, when the magic child of Mary made
his appearance, there was a complete cycle of legends about
him. In the first place he had to be born in Bethlehem because
the prophet Micah of seven hundred years previously had
predicted that. There had to be some reason why a woman
who was expecting a child should travel the long distance
from Nazareth to Bethlehem, which is below Jerusalem; so
there was a story that everyone had to go to be taxed in his
own city, and Joseph, because he was of the house and lineage
of David, had to go. There was no such law or practice known
to the Romans, and no record of any such taxing. It is interesting to note that the legend-makers frequently put in naively
the words, "in order that the prophecy might be fulfilled."
The child was laid in a manger because there was no room
for the family in the inn; and that is believable. But I have
my doubts concerning the shepherds who watched their flocks
by night, and the angel of the Lord who came to them and

told them, "For unto you is born this day in the city of David a Saviour which is Christ the Lord." In *Matthew* we have the story of the three wise men of the East who had been led by a star and had come to worship 'the new King of the Jews.' The jealousy of Herod was aroused, and he wanted to slay this infant, and so an angel came to Joseph in a dream, and they were told to flee with the child to Egypt, and they did so. The three wise men led by the star came to the infant and worshiped him and "presented unto him gifts; gold, frankincense and myrrh. Then Herod, when he saw that he was mocked of the wise men, was exceeding wroth, and sent forth, and slew all the children that were in Bethlehem, and in all the coasts thereof, from two years old and under, according to the time which he had diligently enquired of the wise men." (MATTHEW 2:16)

All this seems to be legend, not history. We know a great deal about the crimes of Herod; they are told about in Josephus. This puppet-king was a bloodthirsty brute, but he never did anything such as slaying "all the children that were in Bethlehem, and in all the coasts thereof, from two years old and under." Such a crime could not have been committed without being known all over the Roman world, and Herod would surely have heard from his Emperor Augustus about it.

Herod died in the year 4 B.C.; but the devout all believe that Jesus was born on December 25th, year 1 of the Christian era. Also it is worth mentioning that the Gospel stories are unhistoric as to both the birth and the death of John the Baptist. Instead of being born just before Jesus he was an elderly man then, a prophet and preacher to Judas of Galilee, leader of the revolt when Herod the Great died. Also, he outlived Jesus by some years, and the story of his being beheaded at the request of Salome, daughter of Herodias and Herod Antipas, is impure fiction; the marriage of this pair, which made such a scandal among the Jews, did not take place until later. The most probable date of the Baptist's death is 36 A.D.

13

We have glanced at the Jewish contribution to the development of Christianity; and now let us take up the Roman contribution. This might be said to have begun with the centurion, commander of a hundred Roman soldiers, who supervised the crucifixion and said, "Truly this man was the Son of God."

Remarks to this effect attributed to Jesus and his followers I take to be legendary, so it might well be that the centurion was the first person in the world who actually gave him this title. It was easy for a Roman centurion to believe in demigods; his religion had a generous supply of them—I don't know if anyone has counted the number. This centurion would have admired especially demigod Hercules, product of a visit to earth by the head god Jupiter and his seduction of a Roman married lady. Hercules was a mighty hero and performed labors such as would be appreciated by a military man; he never talked any nonsense about loving his enemies or turning the other cheek to any smiter.

Another contribution by the Romans was the Pope, both the office and the name. The name comes from the Latin *papa* meaning father, and the office is supposed to have come by direct Apostolic Succession, Jesus appointing Peter, Peter appointing his successor, and so on. The Pope is called the Vicar of Christ, and is a sacred being to all Catholics, possessing divine infallibility when speaking officially on questions of faith and morals. Disbelieve him at your peril, for he is the holder of the power to bind and loose, which means to fasten the guilt of your sins upon you or relieve you of the burden.

Also, the Romans contributed a line of Christian emperors. Emperors were something the Jews never had or wanted. Very certainly Jesus would not have wanted them, and if he had been alive he would have liked them not a bit more than he liked the Emperor Tiberius or his deputy Pontius Pilate, procurator of Judea, who gave way and consented to the crucifixion of an innocent man. "I find no fault in this man," he had said, according to Luke; but the chief priests clamored, "He stirreth up the people, teaching through all Jewry, beginning from Galilee to this place." So finally Pilate gave up and went and washed his hands of the matter. Jesus turned to the wailing women and said, "Daughters of Jerusalem, weep not for me, but weep for yourselves, and for your children. For behold, the days are coming, in the which they shall say, Blessed are the barren, and the wombs that never bear, and the paps which never gave suck. Then shall they begin to say to the mountains, Fall on us; and to the hills, cover us." (LUKE 23:28–30)

14

The Greeks, too, made important contributions to the new faith. They had had a wonderful culture, but that had been centuries ago. Medical men say the decline was due to malaria; historians say it was interstate jealousies and civil wars; economists say it was the operation of those forces which have destroyed every civilization, luxury among the rich and misery and discontent among the poor. Anyhow, many of the Greeks were elegant dilettantes who sometimes earned a good living as slaves, teaching crude insensitive Romans and their children the joys of poetry, music, art, and philosophy. Their thinking was subtle and abstract; they had a genius for metaphysics, a faculty that the Jews lacked.

The Greek influence is obvious in the so-called Fourth Gospel, which is attributed to John, supposedly "the disciple whom Jesus loved." In the course of a long life I have had occasion to consult the Gospels frequently, but after my student days I did not read them through consecutively. I learned in the interim that modern criticism considered the Fourth Gospel to be in a separate class from the other three, called Synoptic. I learned that most theologians agreed that the Fourth Gospel could not have been written by John, the beloved disciple, or indeed by any disciple, but was a much later work.

When I came to reread it I was astonished by what I found, and could hardly believe that anyone had ever imagined it being written by the same kind of person as the authors of *Matthew, Mark,* and *Luke.* These three stories are told by simple, believing Jews; but the fourth is told by a highly educated Greek, who performs a pious service by fitting the Christian story into the philosophical system called neo-Platonism. Plato had taught in Athens four hundred years earlier, and Philo, a Hellenized Jew who lived in Alexandria in the time of Jesus, had absorbed Plato's ideas and adapted them to his over-subtle and decadent age.

Consider the way these four evangelists start. Matthew says, "The book of the generation of Jesus Christ, the son of David, the son of Abraham." That, you can see, is a good Jewish beginning; and it is proof that the writer did not believe that Jesus was born of a virgin, for he gave him a long line of paternal ancestors. Then comes Mark, who says. "The beginning of the Gospel of Jesus Christ, the Son of God; as it is

written in the prophets, behold, I send my messenger before
thy face, which shall prepare thy way before thee. The voice
of one crying in the wilderness, Prepare ye the way of the
Lord, make his paths straight." That, too, is in the spirit of the
old Jewish prophets. Then comes Luke, who is personal and
literary, as you can see: "Forasmuch as many have taken in
hand to set forth in order a declaration of those things which
are most surely believed among us, even as they delivered
them unto us, which from the beginning were eyewitnesses,
and ministers of the word; it seemed good to me also, having
had perfect understanding of all things from the very first,
to write unto thee in order, most excellent Theophilus."

But now comes John, and what a difference! "In the beginning was the Word, and the Word was with God, and the
Word was God. The same was in the beginning with God. All
things were made by Him; and without Him was not anything
made that was made. In Him was life; and the life was the
light of men. And the light shineth in darkness; and the darkness comprehended it not. There was a man sent from God,
whose name was John. The same came for a witness, to bear
witness of the Light, that all men through him might believe.
He was not that Light, but was sent to bear witness of that
Light. That was the true Light, which lighteth every man
that cometh into the world. He was in the world, and the
world was made by Him, and the world knew Him not. He
came unto His own, and His own received Him not." (JOHN
1:1–11)

15

So you see we are not going to learn very much about the
historical Jesus; we are going to learn what this Hellenized
intellectual thinks about Jesus. 'The Word' is the Greek word
Logos, and in English you spell it with a capital, which makes
it important and in fact identifies it with God. Plato called it
the Idea, and that also we spell with a capital. It means that
God is Mind, or the Divine Universal Principle, which may be
true, but has nothing to do with Jesus. For Jesus didn't talk
about Mind, he didn't talk about Principle, or about any
abstractions; he talked about his Heavenly Father. He was
not interested in Mind, but in minds—those of the people
about him and what they were believing. He was trying to
persuade the people he met to think devoutly. He said, "Pray
without ceasing." He said, "Your Heavenly Father knoweth."

He said, "Neither shall they say, 'Lo here! or, lo there!' for, behold, the kingdom of God is within you." (LUKE 17:21)

These things, you see, are simple and concrete. They are meant to be simple, and the simplicity is the essence of them. Jesus must have known that there were Greek-style philosophers in Jewry, and he may have been repudiating them when he said, "Verily I say unto you, Except ye be converted, and become as little children, ye shall not enter into the kingdom of heaven. Whosoever therefore shall humble himself as this little child, the same is greatest in the kingdom of heaven. And whoso shall receive one such little child in my name receiveth me. But whoso shall offend one of these little ones which believe in me, it were better for him that a millstone were hanged about his neck, and that he were drowned in the depth of the sea." (MATTHEW 18:3–6)

But now observe, in the Gospel according to John, how the whole tone is changed. The emphasis is now largely on doctrine, and it is subtle doctrine, and only the educated can understand it. John tells how Jesus answered them, and said, "My doctrine is not mine, but His that sent me." (JOHN 7:16) So John could have doctrine, and in the name of God.

By now there had come to be ceremonies having esoteric significance. The Christians were eating bread and drinking wine, and this is the way that John talks about it, or rather has Jesus talking about it: "Verily, verily, I say unto you, he that believeth on Me hath everlasting life. I am that bread of life. Your fathers did eat manna in the wilderness, and are dead. This is the bread which cometh down from heaven, that a man may eat thereof, and not die. I am the living bread which came down from heaven: if any man eat of this bread, he shall live for ever: and the bread that I will give is My flesh, which I will give for the life of the world." (JOHN 6:47–51)

And when the Jews were bewildered by all this, as well they might be, we hear Jesus: "Verily, verily, I say unto you. Except ye eat the flesh of the Son of Man, and drink His blood, ye have no life in you. Whoso eateth My flesh, and drinketh My blood, hath eternal life; and I will raise him up at the last day. For My flesh is meat indeed, and My blood is drink indeed. He that eateth My flesh, and drinketh My blood, dwelleth in Me, and I in him. As the living Father hath sent Me, and I live by the Father: so he that eateth Me, even he shall live by Me. This is that bread which came down from heaven: not as your fathers did eat manna, and

are dead: he that eateth of this bread shall live for ever."
(JOHN 6:53–58) This, you see, is late church ritual.

16

I don't know how you will find all this, but for me it is the
complete wiping out of the spirit of Jesus, and the substitution
of a theologian. The clergyman friend of my youth had a
study, and in that study were shelves and shelves of books,
mostly bound in black and looking most formidable. I dipped
into them, and perceived that they were dead books and not
for my living mind. I know now that they were derivations of
the mind of this Greek metaphysician who is known to the
Church as St. John, and who succeeded in making Jesus over
into his own image. Read on, for it is the history of the human
mind for many centuries which is being generated here, and
you must understand it, if only to get yourself and other
people out from under its dark shadow.

Jesus is now God, or the Logos, the Word, and, of course
he knows everything. "These words spake Jesus in the treasury, as He taught in the Temple: and no man laid hands on
him; for his hour was not yet come. Then said Jesus again
unto them, 'I go My way, and he shall seek Me, and shall die
in your sins: whither I go, ye cannot come.'" (JOHN 8:30–21)
He is now the Son of God with capital letters, and he hasn't
the least objection to saying so. "If the Son therefore shall
make you free, ye shall be free indeed." (JOHN 8:36) And
again "Jesus said unto them, 'If God were your father, ye
would love Me: for I proceeded forth and came from God;
neither came I of myself, but He sent Me.'"

No more talk about "Why callest thou me good?"! No more
false modesty! "Jesus said unto them, 'Verily, verily, I say
unto you, Before Abraham was, I am.'"

Also the parables have undergone a transformation. No
longer are they simple stories of peasant and desert life. They
are transformed into long discourses. "As the Father knoweth
Me, even so know I the Father: and I lay down My life for the
sheep. And other sheep I have, which are not of this fold: them
also I must bring, and they shall hear My voice; and there
shall be one fold, and one Shepherd. Therefore doth my Father
love Me, because I lay down My life, that I might take it
again. No man taketh it from Me, but I lay it down of Myself. I have power to lay it down, and I have power to take it
again. This commandment have I received of My Father."
(JOHN 10:15–18)

You remember the Jesus who said that "an evil and adulterous generation seeketh after a sign." But now there come voices from Heaven accompanying him, and making it strange indeed that people do not believe in him. He cries, " 'Father, glorify Thy name.' Then came there a voice from heaven, saying, 'I have both glorified it, and will glorify it again.' The people therefore, that stood by, and heard it, said that it thundered: others said, 'An angel spake to Him.' " (JOHN 12:28–29)

Now his time draws near, and he has no doubts, he knows all about it. "Now before the feast of the Passover, when Jesus knew that His hour was come that He should depart out of this world unto the Father, having loved His own which were in the world, He loved them unto the end." (JOHN 13:14)

17

Once more I have to mention the rich young man who called Jesus good master, and he said "Why callest thou me good, there is none good but one, that is God." But see now, what a different tone! "Ye call Me Master and Lord; and you say well, for so I am." (JOHN 13:14)

He is about to die, but he gives us long preachments, all full of doctrine. "Then cometh He to Simon Peter: and Peter saith unto him, 'Lord, dost Thou wash my feet?' Jesus saith to him, 'He that is washed needeth not save to wash his feet, but is clean every whit: and ye are clean, but not all.' For He knew who should betray Him; therefore said He, 'Ye are not all clean.' So after He had washed their feet, and had taken His garments, and was set down again, He said unto them, 'Know ye what I have done to you? ye call Me Master and Lord: and ye say well; for so I am.' " (JOHN 13:6–13)

He is preparing the doctrine of the Trinity; "Three in One and One in Three, Holy, Blessed Trinity,"—so runs the hymn I sang in the Church of the Holy Communion. He says, "But the Comforter, which is the Holy Ghost, whom the Father will send in My name, He shall teach you all things, and bring all things to your remembrance, whatsoever I have said unto you." (JOHN 14:26)

All I can say is, that for me he takes the humanity and interest out of the story of the crucifixion. If the Son knew all these things, it was easy indeed for him to die; but why should he die, since the Father had all power, and could have saved him and all the rest of mankind without going through such an unpleasant procedure? The whole thing becomes a farce and a stupid one. It is all preparation for ritual and priest-craft, and for dreary sermons by the millions, and whole libraries of heavy books bound in black. In his long final speeches Jesus even tells God what to think and to do. He is the first of the million preachers lifting up their voices: "Oh, Lord, Thou knowest."

The seventeenth chapter of John contains twenty-six verses. I quote only the first five so that you may have a sample as a farewell. "These words spake Jesus, and lifted up His eyes to heaven, and said, 'Father, the hour is come; glorify Thy Son, that Thy Son also may glorify Thee: as Thou has given Him power over all flesh, that He should give eternal life to as many as Thou hast given Him. And this is life eternal, that they might know Thee the only true God, and Jesus Christ whom Thou hast sent. I have glorified Thee on the earth: I have finished the work which Thou gavest Me to do. And now, O Father, glorify Thou Me with Thine own Self with the glory which I had with Thee before the world was.' "

18

So much for the Greek influence; and now for that of Persia and Egypt. Ships came from the latter country to Palestine, and the Persians came by caravan routes across the deserts. Both peoples had their religions, and their legends were known to the Romans, and to Jews like the historian Josephus, who served the Romans and made a good thing of it. These legends had pleased great numbers of people, and what could be more natural than for the devotees of a new and unformed faith to take over such ready made material?

The Persians had an ancient sun god named Mithras, who is mentioned in Sanskrit works one or two thousand years before Jesus. His religion came into the Roman Empire about the same time as Christianity, and the two were rivals. The *Encyclopedia Britannica* tells us that "the struggle was the more obstinate because of the resemblances between the two religions, which were so numerous and so close as to be notice-able as early as the second century, causing mutual recrimina-tion."

The Encyclopedia goes on to list these surprising re-semblances: "The fraternal spirit of the first communities, and their humble origin; the connection of their central figures with the sun; the legends of the shepherds with their gifts and adoration; the flood, and the ark; the representation in art of the fiery chariot; the drawing of water from the rock, the

use of bell and candle, holy water and communion; the sacti-
fication of Sunday and of the twenty-fifth of December; the
insistence on moral conduct, the emphasis placed upon ab-
stinence and self-control; the doctrine of heaven and hell, of
primitive revelation, of the mediation of the Logos emanating
from the divine; the atoning sacrifice, the constant warfare between good and evil and the final triumph of the former; the
immortality of the soul, the last judgment, the resurrection of
the flesh, and the fiery destruction of the universe—are some
of the resemblances which, whether real or only apparent, en-
abled Mithraism to prolong its resistance to Christianity."

19

The same extraordinary resemblances are noticed in the case
of Egypt. Here is Gerald Massey, student of Egyptian culture, writing in his book, *The Natural Genesis,* as follows:

"Egypt labored at the portrait (of the Christ) for thousands of years before the Greeks added their finishing touches
to the type of the ever youthful solar god. It was Egypt that
first made the statue live with her own life and humanized her
ideal of the divine. Here was the legend of supreme pity and
self-sacrifice so often told of the canonical Christ. She related
how the God did leave the courts of heaven and come down
as a little child, the infant Horus, born of the Virgin, to whom
he took flesh, or descended into matter, 'crossed the earth as a
substitute' (Ritual, Chapter xlviii), descended into Hades as
vivifier of the dead, their vicarious justifier and redeemer, the
first fruits and leader of the resurrection into eternal life. The
Christian legends were first related of Horus or Osiris, who
was the embodiment of divine goodness, wisdom, truth and
purity; who personated ideal perfection in each sphere of
manifestation and every phase of power."

Alvin Boyd Kuhn, another student of the ancient mytholo-
gies, writes in his book *Who Is This King of Glory?* as follows: "The Christians of the third and fourth centuries were
plagued to destruction by the recurrent appearance of evidence that revealed the disconcerting identity of the Gospel
narrative in many places with incidents in the 'lives' of Horus,
Izdubar, Mithras, Sabazius, Adonis, Witoba, Hercules, Mar-
duk, Krishna, Buddha, and other divine messengers of early
nations. They answered the challenge of this situation with a
desperate allegation that the similarity was the work of the
devil."

Dr. Kuhn goes on to say, "The record is in Egypt. An

Egyptian Jesus—Horus—had raised an Egyptian Lazarus
from the dead at an Egyptian Bethany, with an Egyptian
Mary and Martha present in the scripts of that ancient land
that were extant about five thousand years B.C. And a carving
in relief, depicting scenes of angels announcing from the sky
to the shepherds in the fields a deific advent, of an angel,
Gabriel, foretelling to a virgin that she should be the mother
of the Christos, of the nativity in the cave, of the three sages
kneeling in adoration before the infant deity, had been on the
walls of the temple of Luxor at least seventeen hundred years
B.C. The Virgin Mother had held the divine child in her arms
in zodiacs on temple ceilings for millennia before the Galilean
babe saw the light."

Such is the evidence which has caused some scholars to conclude that Jesus himself is a sun-god myth, and that no such
man ever lived in Palestine. They have not convinced me,
because, as I have said, behind the myths I find no personality,
but in the case of Jesus there is a convincing one. The purpose
of this book is to try to separate the man and his message
from the legends which have been woven into his record. It is
a task which has been atttempted many times, and doubtless
will have to be repeated for many generations.

20

The *Gospel According to John* is followed in the New Testament by the *Acts of the Apostles,* an account of what happened to the followers of Jesus after his death, and how they
proceeded to carry his teachings to the rest of the world. The
authors were all Jews, but in touch with the gentiles. All
scholars, even the orthodox, admit that the writing was late.
There were church traditions and doubtless scraps of records;
there is evidence of such toward the end of the first century.
They were put together early in the second century, and apparently there was a complete text by 150 A.D. All this is
problematical; and it seems strange that God, having such
important messages to give to mankind, should have left the
texts in so dubious a condition.

The *Acts* narrate how Jesus told his disciples that the
Holy Ghost would come upon them; "and when he had spoken
these things, while they beheld, he was taken up; and the
clouds received him out of their sight." So after that he was
in heaven, sending down the Holy Ghost or an angel now and
then to tell them what to do. When they were all together
with one accord in one place, "suddenly there came a sound

from heaven as of a rushing mighty wind, and it filled all the house where they were sitting. And there appeared unto them cloven tongues like as of fire, and it sat upon each of them. And they were all filled with the Holy Ghost, and began to speak with other tongues, as the Spirit gave them utterance." (ACTS 2:2–4)

They were all Galileans, and had known only the Galilean dialect of Aramaic; but now they could speak all kinds of languages. Naturally the multitude was astonished to hear their own tongues, which are carefully listed in *Acts 2:9–11*— at least a dozen. This is what one scholarly author of the Bampton lectures, which I was given to read in my boyhood, considered a 'moderate' miracle. Certainly it was a useful one, and must have helped greatly to spread the new religion. Peter stood up and assured the multitude that they were "not drunken, as you suppose, seeing it is but the third hour of the day." He went on to quote to them the prophet Joel who had told how things like this would happen. "And it shall come to pass afterward, that I will pour out my spirit upon all flesh; and your sons and your daughters shall prophesy, your old men shall dream dreams, your young men shall see visions." (JOEL 2:28)

Peter went on to preach to them, and it turned out that he was just as full of theological doctrine as John. About three thousand were baptized, and many sold their possessions and goods, getting ready for the second coming of Jesus. Peter commanded a lame man to rise up and walk, and the man "entered into the Temple with him, walking and leaping and praising God."

The disciples in those early days "had all things common." They had made the discovery that this was inevitable if you really meant to follow Jesus; it was impossible to keep love for your brethren in your soul if at the same time you were trying to sell them goods at a profit. But 'flesh' was not always equal to this sacrifice. A man named Ananias and his wife Sapphira sold all their possessions, but kept back part of the price; Peter told Ananias that he was lying to the Holy Ghost, and Ananias fell down and gave up his own ghost. About three hours afterward the same thing happened to his wife; she "then fell down straightway at his feet, and yielded up the ghost." So naturally "great fear came upon all the church, and upon as many as heard these things." (ACTS 5:11)

21

The wonders had got a good start, and Jesus was no longer there to forbid his followers to seek after a sign. So when the apostles were put into prison the angel of the Lord came by night and opened the prison doors and brought them forth. There was a young man 'full of prayer' whose name was Stephen, and he began to work miracles. He made a long Jewish speech and the Jews took him out of the city and stoned him; so he became the first martyr.

One of those who witnessed this martyrdom, 'consenting unto it,' was a young Jewish tentmaker named Saul, a Roman citizen. Saul "made havock of the church, entering into every house, and haling men and women committed them to prison." He was so zealous that he went to the Jewish high priest and got a letter of authority so that he could go to Damascus to persecute the Christians who were working there. "As he journeyed, he came near Damascus: and suddenly there shined round about him a light from heaven: and he fell to the earth and heard a voice saying unto him, 'Saul, Saul, why persecutest thou me?' and he said, 'Who art thou, Lord?' And the Lord said, 'I am Jesus whom thou persecutest: it is hard for thee to kick against the pricks.' and he trembling and astonished said, 'Lord, what wilt thou have me to do?' " (ACTS 9:3–5)

Saul was "without sight for three days"; but the Lord came to a disciple in Damascus and told him to go and restore the sight of Saul, and he did so; and Saul was baptized. "And straightway he preached Christ in the synagogues, that he is the Son of God." (ACTS 9:20)

Saul's name was changed to Paul, and he became the most active of the apostles, traveling all over the Roman world; the greater part of *Acts* deals with his adventures. He had been raised in Tarsus, a Greek city of Cilicia, and he had acquired a cosmopolitan outlook. An educated man, he was the one who took up the doctrines of a Rechabite Jew and made them into a universal creed; one which could be spread among gentiles as well as Jews, and ultimately could reach to the ends of the earth.

Paul's conversion took place only two or three years after the crucifixion. He met some of the disciples and spent a couple of weeks with Peter, but he does not seem to have been interested in the personality of Jesus, and tells little about him.

This is taken up by those who wish to prove that Jesus never existed. But I venture the guess that the reason Paul didn't tell more about Jesus is that he didn't like what he found. Christ as martyr and symbol was wonderful and inspiring, but a carpenter of humble origin and appearance, one who had been laid in a manger when he was born and had never since had a place to lay his head—such "flesh and blood," to use Paul's phrase, was surely not good propaganda material.

But to draw from this the conclusion that Paul knew that Jesus was merely an Egyptian and Mythraic symbol seems to me irrational. If there ever was a literal believer on this earth, it was this ex-Pharisee. Discussing the subject of the resurrection he wrote, "And if Christ be not risen, then is our preaching vain, and your faith is also vain." (I CORINTHIANS 15:14) And then again, "And if Christ be not raised, your faith is vain; ye are yet in your sins. Then they also which are fallen asleep in Christ are perished. If in this life only we have hope in Christ, we are of all men most miserable." (I CORINTHIANS 15:17–19) I don't think a man would write like that about an imaginary symbol or legend or myth. In his "Epistle to the Galatians" Paul states, "But other of the apostles saw I none, save James the Lord's brother." Surely one cannot meet the brother of a symbol or legend or myth.

22

The gates between heaven and earth were opened in those extraordinary days, and communications were frequent. The apostles were told that the message of Jesus was to be carried also to the gentiles, and they obeyed this command, and Paul came to be known as 'the apostle to the gentiles.' When Peter was put in prison by the soldiers of Herod Antipas an angel came and opened the prison doors, took off Peter's chains, and set him free. Then Herod was furious and ordered the soldiers killed. He made a speech in which he did not glorify the Lord, and so an angel came down from Heaven and smote him, and "he was eaten of worms, and gave up the ghost."

The apostles had been told that they could work miracles, and they did. One of the miracles Paul worked was to blind a man who mocked at him—presumably this convinced the bystanders. It would seem that the men who spread the Christian legends did not always trouble to conform to the principles of their founder. Concerning all these events we have to say the same thing that we said concerning the miracles of Jesus himself; some may have happened, and others have been misrecollected. Coué, outlining his technique of autosuggestion, always took the precaution to add the words "if it is possible." All miracle workers and miracle tellers should be equally cautious.

Paul went to Macedonia, and there in the city of Philippi was a still more wonderful series of events. Paul was shut up in prison, and he and his companion Silas prayed and sang, and there was a great earthquake, and the foundations of the prison were shaken and all the doors were opened and everyone's bands were loosed. The keeper of the prison was so frightened that he wanted to commit suicide, but Paul persuaded him not to, and converted him. Then they were all let out of prison and departed out of the city. The tale, of course, would help them in the next city.

Paul went to Athens, and out of that visit came a picturesque confrontation of Jewish and Greek cultures: "Now while Paul waited for them at Athens, his spirit was stirred in him, when he saw the city wholly given to idolatry. Therefore disputed he in the synagogue with the Jews, and with the devout persons, and in the market daily with them that met with him. Then certain philosophers of the Epicureans, and of the Stoicks, encountered him. And some said, 'What will this babbler say?' other some, 'He seemeth to be a setter forth of strange gods': because he preached unto them Jesus, and the resurrection. And they took him, and brought him unto Areopagus, saying, 'May we know what this new doctrine, whereof thou speakest, is? for thou bringest certain strange things to our ears: we would know therefore what these things mean.' (For all the Athenians and strangers which were there spent their time in nothing else, but either to tell, or to hear some new thing.) Then Paul stood in the midst of Mars' hill, and said, 'Ye men of Athens, I perceive that in all things ye are too superstitious. For as I passed by, and beheld your devotions, I found an altar with this inscription, TO THE UNKNOWN GOD. Whom, therefore, ye ignorantly worship, Him declare I unto you. God that made the world and all things therein, seeing that He is Lord of heaven and earth, dwelleth not in temples made with hands; neither is worshipped with men's hands, as though He needed any thing, seeing He giveth to all life, and breath, and all things; and hath made of one blood all nations of men for to dwell on all

the face of the earth, and hath determined the times before
appointed, and the bounds of their habitation; that they should
seek the Lord, if haply they might feel after Him, and find
Him, though He be not far from every one of us: for in Him
we live, and move, and have our being; as certain also of your
own poets have said, for we are also His offspring. Forasmuch
then as we are the offspring of God, we ought not to think
that the Godhead is like unto gold, or silver, or stone, graven
by art and man's device. And the times of this ignorance God
winked at; but now commandeth all men every where to repent; because He hath appointed a day, in the which He will
judge the world in righteousness by that man whom He hath
ordained; whereof He hath given assurance unto all men, in
that He hath raised him from the dead.' And when they heard
of the resurrection of the dead, some mocked: and others said,
'We will hear thee again of this matter.' So Paul departed
from among them." (ACTS 17:16–33)

23

Paul, as you can see, was an able man; the ablest that early
Christianity produced. He is described as being small but
sturdy, bow-legged and bald. For something like thirty-five
years he traveled over the Roman world, preaching "Christ
crucified" and founding churches wherever he went. The last
we hear of him, he was a prisoner in Rome; it is not known
definitely what happened to him, but it is believed that he was
executed. As a Roman citizen he was entitled to die by being
beheaded with a sword. But there was no way that even the
Romans could end the life of his words.

We have, in the New Testament, a dozen letters supposed
to have been written to his churches and friends. They are
called the *Epistles of Paul,* and are probably the earliest in
date of any Christian documents we have. Paul's authorship
has been disputed; but I feel about several of these letters as
I feel about the stories concerning Jesus: there is a personality
in them. If Paul did not write the *Epistle to the Romans* and
the two to the Corinthians, they are surely the work of someone who knew his spirit and his mind. The man is here, a man
of tremendous energy, profound conviction, moral passion
and eloquence; a man who has been blessed with a revelation,
and who has one purpose in life, to spread the precious message to all who can be persuaded to listen.

He has groups of followers, probably small in numbers,
whom he addresses as "Dearly beloved brethren." He instructs

them, he exhorts them, he scolds them, he calls them 'children'
and 'little children.' He tells them about his adventures and
experiences; he warns them about the traps set for them; he
intervenes in their quarrels and tries to settle them; he is
schoolmaster, guardian, and guide. He tells them their sins,
which are quite terrifying. He gives you a list of them, sparing
nothing:

"Now the works of the flesh are manifest, which are these;
Adultery, fornication, uncleanness, lasciviousness, idolatry,
witchcraft, hatred, variance, emulations, wrath, strife, sedi-
tions, heresies, envyings, murders, drunkenness, revellings,
and such like; of the which I tell you before, as I have also
told you in time past, that they which do such things shall not
inherit the kingdom of God. But the fruit of the Spirit is love,
joy, peace, longsuffering, gentleness, goodness, faith, meek-
ness, temperance: against such there is no law. And they that
are Christ's have crucified the flesh with the affections and
lusts. If we live in the Spirit, let us also walk in the Spirit. Let
us not be desirous of vain glory, provoking one another, envy-
ing one another." (GALATIANS 5:19–26)

He sends messages to the various members by name, re-
minds them of their encounters, and tells them what to do. To
me the letters seem lifelike and convincing, and inspire me
with both respect and affection for this ardent preacher of
righteousness. (I remember the story of a Catholic priest who
objected to the non-ecclesiastical way of referring to him, and
said that if we weren't willing to call him St. Paul, we might
at least call him Mr. Paul.)

24

It is fascinating, but at the same time distressing, to see this
Roman citizen taking the warm, personal message of Jesus
and supplying it with a theological system and a set of
dogmas. Paul tells us, in his *Epistle to the Galatians*, how,
when it pleased God to reveal His Son to him, he "conferred
not with flesh and blood, but went into Arabia." He uses the
term loosely, meaning the desert which lies east of the Sea of
Galilee and the Jordan. It was the land which had been the
home of the young Yeshu, and it is curious to think that Paul
may have gone there in order to meet the tribe and see what
they were like. He prayed in the same places where Yeshu
had prayed, but he did not bring out the same message. It
would appear that he did not have the direct relation with his
Heavenly Father; he had been converted through Jesus, and

Jesus was his mediator and intercessor. He is perfectly convinced that Jesus was the Son of God, and is now sitting at the right hand of the Father. He sees that mankind is sunk in sin, and he accepts the ancient Hebrew legend that it was all due to the episode in the Garden of Eden. "For as in Adam all die, even so in Christ shall all be made alive."

There you have the Pauline theology in one sentence. In it you have all history, all philosophy, all religion—you might even say all science and all knowledge of any consequence to you. Mankind was lost and doomed to hell, but Jesus Christ came down from heaven and offered himself as a blood sacrifice to redeem you. If you believe on him, be baptized and have your sins washed away, abandon your sinful ways, and pray to him—thus your soul is saved, and in the end you are taken to his bosom. Such is the story, and it is as simple as can be. Paul rings a hundred changes on it, and pours out extraordinary eloquence upon it. He is a master of language, even if his Greek was not perfect. "O wretched man that I am!" he exclaims. "Who shall deliver me from the body of this death?" How many millions of preachers have repeated these words!

He is almost as successful as his master Jesus in making phrases which will become familiar quotations. He warns the Galatians, "Be not deceived; God is not mocked: for whatsoever a man soweth, that shall he also reap." (GALATIANS 6:7) He tells us, "The Lord loveth a cheerful giver." One of his finest chapters is the thirteenth in the "First Epistle to the Corinthians." Anyone who wants to know the man must read it entire:

"Though I speak with the tongues of men and of angels, and have not charity, I am become as sounding brass, or a tinkling cymbal. And though I have the gift of prophecy, and understand all mysteries, and all knowledge; and though I have all faith, so that I could remove mountains, and have not charity, I am nothing. And though I bestow all my goods to feed the poor, and though I give my body to be burned, and have not charity, it profiteth me nothing. Charity suffereth long, and is kind; charity envieth not; charity vaunteth not itself, is not puffed up, doth not behave itself unseemly, seeketh not her own, is not easily provoked, thinketh no evil; rejoiceth not in iniquity, but rejoiceth in the truth; beareth all things, believeth all things, hopeth all things, endureth all things. Charity never faileth; but whether there be prophecies, they shall fail; whether there be tongues, they shall cease;

whether there be knowledge, it shall vanish away. For we
know in part, and we prophesy in part. But when that which
is perfect is come, then that which is in part shall be done
away. When I was a child, I spake as a child, I understood as
a child, I thought as a child: but when I became a man, I put
away childish things. For now we see through a glass, darkly;
but then face to face: now I know in part; but then shall
I know even as also I am known. And now abideth faith,
hope, charity, these three; but the greatest of these is charity."

25

This is magnificent preaching; and equally good is the message he sends to the Romans—meaning thereby the Chris-
tianized Jews and gentiles in Rome. He tells them:
"I beseech you therefore, brethren, by the mercies of God,
that ye present your bodies a living sacrifice, holy, acceptable
unto God, which is your reasonable service. And be not con-
formed to the world: but be ye transformed by the renewing
of your mind, that ye may prove what is that good, and acceptable, and perfect, will of God. Let love be without dis-
simulation. Abhor that which is evil; cleave to that which is
good. Be kindly affectioned one to another with brotherly
love; in honour preferring one another; not slothful in business; fervent in spirit; serving the Lord; rejoicing in hope;
patient in tribulation; continuing instant in prayer; dis-
tributing to the necessity of saints; given to hospitality.
Bless them which persecute you: bless, and curse not. Rejoice
with them that do rejoice, and weep with them that weep. Be
of the same mind one toward another. Mind not high things,
but condescend to men of low estate. Be not wise in your own
conceits. Recompense to no man evil for evil. Provide things
honest in the sight of all men. If it be possible, as much as
lieth in you, live peaceably with all men. Dearly beloved,
avenge not yourselves, but rather give place unto wrath: for it
is written, 'Vengeance is mine; I will repay, saith the Lord.'
Therefore if thine enemy hunger, feed him; if he thirst, give
him drink: for in so doing thou shalt heap coals of fire on his
head. Be not overcome of evil, but overcome evil with good."
(ROMANS 12:1-2 . . . 9–21)
All this is exactly in the spirit of Jesus; but there are other
aspects of Jesus which apparently had less meaning to Paul.
We find in him little of the eschatology, the coming end of the
world. We find nothing of the social rebellion; Paul was a

Roman citizen and son of a Roman citizen. In his childhood
and youth he had never known hunger or want, and had none
of the bitterness against the rich that Jesus showed. In his
Epistle to the Ephesians he orders, "Servants, be obedient to
them that are your masters according to the flesh, with fear
and trembling, in singleness of your heart, as unto Christ."
(EPHESIANS 6:5)

As for women he orders, "Wives, submit yourselves unto
your own husbands, as unto the Lord. For the husband is the
head of the wife, even as Christ is the head of the Church: and
he is the saviour of the body. Therefore as the Church is subject unto Christ, so let the wives be to their own husbands in
every thing." (EPHESIANS 5:22–24) And still more explicitly:
"Let the woman learn in silence with all subjection. But I
suffer not a woman to teach, nor to usurp authority over the
man, but to be in silence. For Adam was first formed, then
Eve. And Adam was not deceived, but the woman being deceived was in the transgression." (I TIMOTHY 2:11–14)

As to the question of government, it is obvious that Paul
could not have preached resistance to the Romans, or even
hinted at it, and remained free to travel over the Roman Empire as he did for thirty-five years. Jesus had talked his
proletarian sentiments in Galilee, a place not much regarded
by the Romans; but when he went to Jerusalem and tried it,
he paid for the experiment with his life. Paul apparently paid
in the end; but he lasted a long time, by making his sociologi-
cal doctrines entirely satisfactory to the Romans. In his letter
to Titus he tells this disciple to "put them (the congregation)
in mind to be subject to principalities and powers, to obey
magistrates, to be ready to every good work."

26

How different when we turn over a few pages of our New
Testament and come to James, the brother of Jesus. This was
a Rechabite man who had known hunger and want, and who
shared the social feelings of the ancient prophets. He had been
slow to follow Jesus, but had become one of the original
Twelve, and is known to history as James the Good, the Just,
the Righteous. Listen to him now: "Go to now, ye rich men,
weep and howl for your miseries that shall come upon you.
Your riches are corrupted, and your garments are moth-eaten.
Your gold and silver is cankered; and the rust of them shall be
a witness against you, and shall eat your flesh as it were fire.
Ye have heaped treasure together for the last days. Behold,

the hire of the labourers who have reaped down your fields, which is of you kept back by fraud, crieth: and the cries of them which have reaped are entered into the ears of the Lord of Sabaoth. Ye have lived in pleasure on the earth, and been wanton; ye have nourished your hearts, as in a day of slaughter. Ye have condemned and killed the just; and he doth not resist you. Be patient therefore, brethren, unto the coming of the Lord. Behold, the husbandman waiteth for the precious fruit of the earth, and hath long patience for it, until he receive the early and latter rain. Be ye also patient; stablish your hearts: for the coming of the Lord draweth nigh." (JAMES 5:1–8)

Here again, you see, is the expectation of the early end of the world. After reading the passages above you will not be surprised to hear that this desert rebel was put to death by stoning—on the orders of the Sadducean high priest.

27

There is an interesting point to be mentioned in connection with this brother of Jesus. I so referred to him in my novelette, "Our Lady," and received a letter from a Catholic lady stating flatly, "Jesus had no brother." Obviously it is a matter of grave offense to the Catholics that their Blessed Virgin should have had any children either before or after Jesus. She remained the Holy One, and in course of time the Church adopted a declaration to the effect that she too had been immaculately conceived; also that she was taken bodily up to heaven. Just recently the Pope has established this last as the official dogma, which must be received under penalty of heresy. So there she sits as the Queen of Heaven, and, of course, a Virgin Queen. The Catholics all pray to her to intercede with God; in effect this constitutes her a goddess—although the Catholics vehemently deny this. Personally, I cannot see why, if there is a Man-God, there cannot also be a Woman-God.

What is the evidence as to her family? We have already seen how in *Galatians 1:19* Paul states "But other of the apostles saw I none, save James the Lord's brother." Josephus, the historian, writing a generation after Jesus, states in his *Antiquities* how Annas the high priest lost no time in bringing before the Sanhedrin "one by name James, the brother of Jesus who was called the Messiah." We read also about him in some of the uncanonical gospels, notably the *Gospel of the Ebionites.* This was an early sect of Christians which was repressed, and James the brother of Jesus was the first of its leaders. It was an ascetic sect, like the Essenes, and Eusebius, an early Church Father, tells us that James lived an abnormally ascetic life and spent all his time praying in the Temple. It is interesting to note that the *Gospel of the Ebionites* says not a word about the virgin birth; which would seem to indicate that James took no stock in that tale. The family knew!

According to the New Testament, Jesus had four brothers; James, Joses, Judah and Simeon. We know that the grandsons of Judah were persecuted by the Emperor Domitian. It is Clement of Alexandria, one of the early Church Fathers, who speaks of James as "the Just," and says he remained an orthodox follower of Judaism, observing all the ceremonial laws. Inside the Church he fought against Paul on this point.

When Jesus at the beginning of his mission went into the synagogue at Nazareth, the people said as follows: "'Is not this the carpenter's son? is not his mother called Mary? and his brethren, James, and Joses, and Simon, and Judas? and his sisters, are they not all with us? Whence then hath this man all these things?' And they were offended in him. But Jesus said unto them, 'A prophet is not without honour, save in his own country, and in his own house.' And he did not many mighty works there because of their unbelief." (MATTHEW 13:55–58)

The brothers of Jesus are mentioned also in *Matthew 12:46–47:* "While he yet talked to the people, behold, his mother and his brethren stood without, desiring to speak with him. Then one said unto him, 'Behold, thy mother and thy brethren stand without, desiring to speak with thee.'" The same story of his mother and brethren "standing without" is in *Mark 3:31.* The story of the brothers and sisters coming to see him is found in *Matthew 13:56,* and is repeated in *Mark 6:3.* If you want to know how the orthodox evade the plain meaning of these texts, I refer you to the old-time Concordance to the Bible which I am using. It dates from 1701, and explains that the words "brothers" and "sisters" can also mean 'cousins.' It does not say whether, when Paul wrote that he met James, the brother of Jesus, he meant that he was meeting a cousin. The Greek word for brothers is *adelphoi* and for sisters is *adelphai.* We are familiar with this in *Philadelphia,* which means 'place of brotherly love.' The Greek for cousins is *suggeveis,* and is found in *Luke 1:58.* The reader may judge for himself the likelihood of these words being confused.

28

One more of the twelve apostles requires our special attention; that is Simon Peter, one of the two fishermen whom Jesus met by the Lake of Galilee; he told them to come with him and he would make them 'fishers of men.' In the Bible story Peter is sometimes called Simon; once he is called Cephas, which is the Hebrew equivalent of Peter. In Aramaic, the language which he spoke, his name was Shimeon Kepha. As I have mentioned earlier, this word *kepha-cephas-petros* means rock, and caused Jesus to make the pun: "Thou art Peter, and upon this rock I will build my church; and the gates of hell shall not prevail against it. And I will give unto thee the keys of the kingdom of heaven: and whatsoever thou shalt bind on earth shall be bound in heaven: and whatsoever thou shalt loose on earth shall be loosed in heaven.' "

We have discussed this previously, but I repeat because it is of crucial importance. It seems to me that to call any man 'the Son of the living God' is something which could never have entered the mind of a Jewish fisherman, and no one would ever have dared to make such a statement to Jesus. I believe that this text got into the Gospels quite late, when the Church was already well established. The idea of giving to a mortal man the power to bind and loose sins would have seemed to Jesus so blasphemous as to be unspeakable.

What was the character of this man to whom the awful powers were supposed to be entrusted? We have seen that Jesus once called him 'Satan' (MATTHEW 16:23) (The pious Alexander Cruden, bookseller to Her Majesty Queen Anne, who published my Concordance, explains to me that 'satan' is a mere Hebrew word and means 'antagonist'.) We are told how, when Christ was arrested and in peril of death, Peter three times denied that he knew him.

Soon after the crucifixion there developed a prolonged quarrel between Peter and Paul. Peter was a conservative Jew, who wished to preserve the practices of the Jewish Law. Paul, the apostle to the gentiles, did not propose to require gentile converts to be circumcized, and he was willing to sit down with them at meals. Peter opposed both these practices with fury. James, the brother of Jesus, sided with Peter, and Paul tells about it in the second chapter of *Galatians*. He is bitter, and speaks of "false brethren brought in, who came in privily to spy out our liberty which we have in Christ Jesus, that they might bring us into bondage." He says dryly that they "seemed to be somewhat in conference," and also he speaks of "James, Cephas (that is Peter), and John, who seemed to be pillars." He goes on to say that "when Peter was come to Antioch, I withstood him to the face, because he was to be blamed." Then he adds, "I saw that they walked not uprightly according to the truth of the Gospel." (GALATIANS 2:14)

29

The consequences of this doctrinal quarrel were beyond any imagining of the men who took part in it. It has continued down through nineteen centuries, and is still going on between tens of millions of men. Before discussing it, let us see what were the teachings of this man who by a false text inserted in the Gospel has been made the keeper of the keys of heaven, and endowed with power to admit men to eternal bliss or consign them to eternal torment. (That is what "binding and loosing" means.) The Holy Catholic Church took him up, and adopted him as the first of its popes. All their power comes from him. And why? Of what use was he to them?

The answer is found in the two epistles of the New Testament attributed to Peter. The first begins as follows: "Peter, an apostle of Jesus Christ, to the strangers scattered throughout Pontus, Galatia, Cappadocia, Asia, and Bithynia, elect according to the foreknowledge of God the Father, through sanctification of the Spirit, unto obedience and sprinkling of the blood of Jesus Christ: Grace unto you, and peace, be multiplied. Blessed be the God and Father of our Lord Jesus Christ, which according to his abundant mercy hath begotten us again unto a lively hope by the resurrection of Jesus Christ from the dead, to an inheritance incorruptible, and undefiled, and that fadeth not away, reserved in heaven for you, who are kept by the power of God through faith unto salvation ready to be revealed in the last time. Wherein ye greatly rejoice, though now for a season, if need be, ye are in heaviness through manifold temptations: that the trial of your faith, being much more precious than of gold that perisheth, though it be tried with fire, might be found unto praise and honour and glory at the appearing of Jesus Christ: whom having not seen, ye love; in whom, though now ye see him not, yet believing, ye rejoice with joy unspeakable and full of glory: receiving the end of your faith, even the salvation of your souls." (I PETER 1:1–9)

From this you will see that he was a wordy ex-fisherman;

and also that he has the Church doctrine all ready to be handed down through the centuries. I am guessing that he never saw these words, but that they were written for him by his followers a century or two later, after the Church had got well started. If I were to call them ghost-writers, it might not be a very good pun.

A few verses further we find him telling his 'strangers' how to pass their time. "And if ye call on the Father, who without respect of persons judgeth according to every man's work, pass the time of your sojourning here in fear: forasmuch as ye know that ye were not redeemed with corruptible things, as silver and gold, from your vain conversation received by tradition from your fathers; but with the precious blood of Christ, as of a lamb without blemish and without spot." (I PETER 1:17–19)

In the next chapter we find him saying, "Submit yourselves to every ordinance of man for the Lord's sake: whether it be to the king, as supreme; or unto governors, as unto them that are sent by him for the punishment of evil-doers, and for the praise of them that do well. For so is the will of God, that with well doing ye may put to silence the ignorance of foolish men: as free, and not using your liberty for a cloke of maliciousness, but as the servants of God. Honour all men. Love the brotherhood. Fear God. Honour the king." (I PETER 2:13–17)

A little later we find him saying, as Jesus said, "But the end of all things is at hand: be ye therefore sober, and watch unto prayer." (I PETER 4:7) He warns you, "Be sober, be vigilant; because your adversary the devil, as a roaring lion, walketh about, seeking whom he may devour." (I PETER 5:8) Again he warns: "But the day of the Lord will come as a thief in the night; in the which the heavens shall pass away with a great noise, and the elements shall melt with fervent heat, the earth also and the works that are therein shall be burned up." (2 PETER 3:10) And he holds out the great reward, "And when the chief Shepherd shall appear, ye shall receive a crown of glory that fadeth not away." (I PETER 5:4)

There, you see, is everything that it takes to build a Holy Church. There is everything that priests, bishops, archbishops, cardinals and popes could ask to give them authority over human souls, and enable them to take charge of the world's affairs. There will be a colossal organization based upon that dreadful power of sending souls into eternal hell fire; and all the sins of that Church and of its prelates shall be washed away in the blood of Jesus—for with marvelous prophetic foresight Peter tells them that "Charity shall cover the multitude of sins."

So we can see—with the wisdom of hindsight—what is going to happen. There is a quarrel between Peter and Paul, and Peter wins out. He becomes the head of the Church in Jerusalem, and lives to a ripe old age. While Paul wanders here and there preaching to little groups about individual righteousness and personal salvation, Peter is building an ecclesiastical machine. The result is that Paul's writings were suppressed for more than a hundred years. The early Church Father Tertullian, a bitter fanatic, calls him "the apostle to the heretics." Paul's story ends abruptly with him a prisoner in Rome.

But Peter's Church rises and thrives and puts down all the heretics. The bigger it becomes the more firmly it relies upon priestcraft and the more corruptions it develops. Rites and ceremonies are invented and they become full of magical power. Texts are written down and become the Word of God. Churches by the thousand are raised, crucifixes by millions are carved and blessed and worshiped. It is the Holy Catholic Church, and its motto is *semper eadem,* which means "always the same."

30

The last book of the New Testament is called *The Revelation of St. John the Divine.* We find the writer angry against various kinds of wrong believers; and after he has called them bad names and threatened punishments, he begins to tell visions of beasts with many horns, and scarlet women drunken with the blood of the saints, and so on for ten or twelve thousand words. I leave this work to those who can make something of it.

But I make a great deal of bewildered souls, born into a time of torment, hungering and thirsting after righteousness and groping their way toward a new light. Jesus had given them an impulse of the spirit, and they were possessed by it and determined to spread it; in order to do so they gave up comfort and worldly security, and risked imprisonment, torture, and cruel death. It is easy for us with our superior knowledge to smile over their credulity, but it would be more becoming of us to see that we equal them in moral earnestness and resolution.

Jesus had talked about seeds that fell upon good ground and

brought forth fruit. He had planted such seeds, and they were growing. Day and night the disciples and their followers were preaching and praying, arguing and pleading and making converts. A century is easy to say, but it takes a long time happening, and in the course of a century of this tireless activity the new faith was spread throughout the Roman world. At the outset the converts were mostly Jewish, and they followed Jewish models in all their procedures. Their gathering places were still called synagogues, and the conservative among them taught the idea that Jesus had not meant to rescind Jewish Law, but merely to end abuses in its observance.

There were Jews scattered in every city and town throughout the Roman world. The gentiles began to come into the movement, and in course of time they took over and began to impose their ideas upon the new creed. That was how the Greek, Roman, Egyptian, Gothic, and Persian influences crept in. Wherever the new religion came it took on the practices and the color of the primitive religions of the converts. There is a book about Mexico called *Idols Behind Altars*, by Anita Brenner, and the title describes a literal condition to be found in that country: the Indians build a Christian altar with the crucifix and all the other trappings, and then behind it they hid an image of one of their ancient Mayan gods. So it is that the Christians have rites, ceremonies and legends so closely resembling those of the old-time sun gods. So it is that we have an Easter named after the Anglo-Saxon goddess of spring, with eggs and bunnies and other relics of the pagan fertility rites of the vernal equinox.

31

At first the new faith lived by tradition; since most of its members were illiterate they did not need writing. Vellum manuscripts were costly, and most of the followers of the creed were poor. But gradually the holy words came to be written out. Tradition tells us that the *Logia*, which means words, were written down by Matthew in Hebrew. His Hebrew name was Mattathiyahu, and he was otherwise known as Halphi the Levite; he was a Jew, a tax collector for the Romans in the town of Capernaum, which had a customs house; Jesus is said to have visited him there. In those days a tax collector was the next thing to a murderer in the eyes of the Jews; he was allowed a share of his collections, and the system was full of extortion. In the Bible the name used is 'publican,' and the

Pharisees asked Jesus why he persisted in consorting with publicans and sinners. He gave them one of his humorous retorts: "They that are whole have no need of the physician, but they that are sick: I came not to call the righteous, but sinners to repentance."

The *Logia* were written down and widely circulated; but, except for one fragment on Egyptian papyrus, they have not come down to us. There was then, according to the belief of present-day scholars, an early version of Mark, a sort of skeletonized account or sketch; it is referred to in modern criticism as 'Q,' from the German word *Quelle*, or source. This was elaborated into the *Gospel According to Mark*, and the Matthew and Luke Gospels were elaborated from that. The *Logia* it is believed, were made into the *Sermon on the Mount* and other discourses. Those who put the texts together would write that Jesus was followed by a multitude, or he went up onto a hill, or into a synagogue to preach, and then they would put in a bunch of these sayings. So the story was given life.

It is to be noted that these four Gospels are not headed *The Gospel of St. Matthew*, etc., but in each case 'according to.' In other words it is the Gospel as each of these evangelists were believed to have preached and taught it. The texts were written in Greek. Up to that time practically all the Christians were Greek-speaking subjects of the Roman Empire, and those among them who were literate were offended by the crudity of style of the Mark Gospel. To a less degree this was true of the writings of Paul, although he was supposed to be an educated man.

The nearest we can come to a contemporary statement as to the origin of the texts is that of Eusebius, in his *Ecclesiastical History*, Book 6, Chapter 14, in which he reports that the people who heard Peter "requested Mark, who remembered well what he (Peter) had said, to reduce these things to writing . . . which when Peter understood, he neither directly hindered nor encouraged it." This must have been in Peter's old age. We are told that at that time he became helpless, and had the humiliation of having to be waited upon by others. We may doubt if any one of the four evangelists ever saw the record which is 'according to' him.

As to the dates when these Gospels came into existence, you may find a variety of opinions, usually determined by the preconceptions of the writer. Since I myself am not an authority, I take the dates which I find in the most recent edition of the

Encyclopedia Britannica. The article on the Bible, New Testament Canon, carries the initials of Rev. John Martin Creed, Canon of Ely (Church of England). He states: "Our inquiries will show us that by the end of the 2nd century the New Testament was already complete in idea, though it was not until the 4th century that the exact limits of the Canon were finally and firmly drawn." (There being two kinds of 'Canon' in the above, I explain for the benefit of the uninitiated that one kind is a collection of holy books received as inspired, and the other kind is a church dignitary, usually attached to a cathedral). The point to be noted is that, by the statement of an orthodox scholar, for more than a century and a half after the death of Jesus his actions and teachings were left to the chances of transmission by word of mouth, or by scraps of writing handed down by persons unknown and who had their own ideas of what should be in the record.

The earliest written record which we possess at the present time dates from the fourth century, and we have only two of these, codexes on vellum. There are a few earlier fragments which have been found in Egypt, where the climate is favorable to the survival of manuscripts. That means that for three hundred years after the death of Jesus, his words and actions were subject to revision by pious interpolators. The Greek and Latin manuscripts of the fourth century are all different, and it wasn't until 483 A.D. that Jerome's "standard revision" was adopted and the Gospels became the 'Word of God.'

32

As to the forgeries, you do not have to take my word, you can have the word of St. Iraeneus, Bishop of Lyons at the end of the second century, that there were "a multitude of Gospels" in his day. You may read in the *Catholic Encyclopedia*, Vol. 5, Page 10, the complaint of Bishop Dionysius that his writings "have been falsified by the apostles of the devil; no wonder that the Scriptures were falsified by such persons." The *Catholic Encyclopedia*, Vol. 4, Page 498, admits that it was the custom of the scribes to lengthen out here and there to harmonize passages, or to add their own explanatory material. This authority concedes that "It is the public character of all divines to mold and bend the sacred oracles till they comply with their own fancy, spreading them . . . like a curtain, closing together or drawing them back as they please."

There have come down to us the *Clementine Homilies*, an

Epistle from Peter to James, and in this Peter says, as follows:
"For some of the converts of the gentiles have rejected the
preaching through me in accordance with the Law, having accepted a certain lawless and babbling doctrine of the enemy.
These same people have attempted while I am still alive by
various interpolations to transform my words unto the over-
throw of the Law; as though I also thought thus but did not
preach it openly: which be far from me . . . But they pro-
fessing somehow to know my mind, attempt to expound the
words they heard from me more wisely than I who spoke
them, telling those who are instructed by them that this is my
meaning, which I never thought of. But if they venture such
falsehoods while I am still alive, how much more when I am
gone will those who come after me dare to do so!" The *Encyclopedia Britannica* presumes that the 'enemy' whose 'lawless and babbling doctrine' troubled Peter so greatly is none
other than Paul. In other words, this is a part of the Peter-Paul
controversy previously referred to.

33

This system of forgeries continued on down through the centuries. One of the most elaborate examples had to do with the
Sibylline books of the Greeks. These held the prophecies of the
Greek oracles, who were considered inspired and whose words
had been carefully preserved. The Christian propagandists
took these up and modified them, putting in all sorts of texts
to prove that the Greek prophetesses had foreseen the coming
of Jesus, and all the miracles he wrought, and the religion he
established.

Kuhn's *Who Is This King of Glory* lists many such instances. "Lorenzo Valla in 1440 first revealed the forgery of
the *Donation of Constantine*. The Symmachian forgeries are
confessed by the *Catholic Encyclopedia*. Voltaire pronounced
the *False Decretals of Isidore* 'the boldest and most magnificent forgery which has deceived the world for centuries.'
They appeared suddenly in the ninth century, and in them
the popes of the first three centuries are made to quote documents which did not appear until the fourth and fifth century;
they are full of anachronisms.

"Then comes the sorry recital of lists of deceptions concerning sacred relics, starting with those of the person of
Jesus, his bones, his garments, utensils used by him, the cross,
nails, bottles of his blood, and also of Mary's nursing milk,
etc. etc., which are so obviously fraudulent that one would

think that the ecclesiastical system which either forged them, or winked at their exploitation, would blush at the record. The *Catholic Encyclopedia* does confess the tolerance of 'the pious beliefs' which have helped to further Christianity, and the general indulgence toward all the fatuous superstitions connected with relics, saints, healing, and the rest."

One of the earliest documents we have after the *Epistles of Paul* is from St. Ignatius, Bishop of Antioch, where according to the *Acts* the disciples were first called Christians. This was at the end of the first century, and we find that the Church now has a bishop, deacons and presbyters. The apostles were all dead and priests were needed for ceremonies; a complete Church system came into being. Faith gave place to obedience; the Jewish Law was replaced by the priest and his authority. The priest had been interposed between God and man, and held the power of salvation. The ceremony of the Mass had taken the place of the doctrine or sermon as the main reliance of Christians.

By the second century this development had been completed. By the third century the organization was calling itself the Catholic Church, meaning that it covered all the world. It was, no doubt, at that time that the paragraphs were inserted in which Jesus told Peter that he was the rock.

34

From the beginning of the Church's history there was quarreling over doctrine, and the splitting off of heretical sects. Preceding Christianity had been Gnosticism, a Greek mystery religion derived from the sun-god worship. Paul, having a Greek education, brought a good deal of Gnosticism into the new faith and won many converts from that sect. One of these was a wealthy shipowner, who must have been a considerable conquest for a humble tentmaker. Marcion was this man's name, and he became a devoted disciple and propagandist for Paul. When the ideas of Paul met their defeat in the struggle with Peter, Marcion broke off and founded a sect of his own, which gained many converts and lasted for a century or two. Then there was Donatism in Africa, and Arianism in Alexandria, and also Semi-Arianism, and Nestorians and Monophysites in the East; there were active Manichaeans, and a Pelagian sect which had considerable influence. In short, the saints of the true faith were plagued by endless uprisings of Satan. To tell what these groups believed and what the quarrels were about would bore any modern reader. Let one example suffice: there were homoousians and there were homoiousians. You will have to examine the two words carefully to discover the difference; but it was of vast importance to the believers, for one meant that the Son was of the same essence as the Father, while the other meant that he was only of *like* essence. That the Church machine of Peter won out in these doctrinal struggles was precisely because it had become a machine. You can see from Peter's teachings which I have quoted, how he was the one best fitted to win. Submission was needed, and he had ordained it; fear was needed, and he could inspire it, because he had the power to send his opponents to hell. Converts were made among the rich, and that made the new faith respectable. It proved to be an excellent faith from their point of view, because it taught the poor obedience and submission; it concentrated their attention upon heaven, and left this world to the powerful who already had it. Much later there was a celibate clergy, which meant that the Church could become really rich. There were monasteries and nunneries as early as the fourth century.

What this new religion was going to teach was laid down in a document known as the *Apostles' Creed,* believed to have been dictated by them. Fragments of it began to appear in the second century after Christ, but the whole was not completed until about 500 A.D. It is accepted by both Western and Eastern Churches, with slight variations. As a little boy in the Protestant Episcopal Church of America I learned it by heart. I take it from my *Book of Common Prayer:*

"I believe in God the Father Almighty, Maker of Heaven and earth: And in Jesus Christ, His only Son our Lord: Who was conceived by the Holy Ghost, Born of the Virgin Mary: Suffered under Pontius Pilate: Was crucified, dead, and buried: He descended into hell; The third day He rose again from the dead: He ascended into Heaven: And sitteth on the right hand of God the Father Almighty: From thence he shall come to judge the quick and the dead. I believe in the Holy Ghost: The holy Catholic Church: The Communion of Saints: The Forgiveness of sins: The Resurrection of the body: And the Life everlasting. Amen."

The little boy who grew up to write this book recited this creed hundreds of times, and with deep reverence; but he never managed to figure out whether "Thency" (thence he) was a person or a place, and who or what was coming from him or it.

35

So far we have been following the story of the spirit of Jesus through Christian sources. It is time now to glimpse the development through the eyes of those opposed to the new religion. The Roman historian Tacitus, writing at the beginning of the second century, tells of the burning of Rome and implies that the Christians were responsible for it. He speaks of them with dislike and says, "Christus, from whom they derived their name, was condemned to death in the reign of Tiberius by the procurator Pontius Pilate." The Roman historian Suetonius, writing about the same time, speaks of the tumults in Rome, and says that "the Emperor banished from Rome the Jews who made great tumult because of Chrestus."

Also we have a letter written by the younger Pliny, who was proconsul of the province of Bithynia to the Emperor Trajan in the year 111. He describes Christianity as a popular movement, but doesn't understand the nature of it. He says they sing a sacred hymn in which they speak of Christus as if he was God. You see that about as late as three-quarters of a century after the crucifixion these educated Roman gentlemen found this strange movement worthy only of disdain—except when there was a possibility that the fanatics might have set fire to the capital city of the empire.

Next, the Jews. Many of those who did not accept Jesus hated him, and as time passed and his movement became more alien to Judaism, the hostility became mutual. So we face here the same problem of textual criticism as with Christian documents. The Jews wanted to ridicule Jesus, so they interpolated in their old documents stories and remarks that served that purpose. Dr. Joseph Klausner, author of "Jesus of Nazareth," has given a fair and intelligent study of these ancient documents, and sums up the evidence they provide as follows:

"There are reliable statements that his name was Yeshu'a of Nazareth, that he practiced 'sorcery' (i.e. performed miracles, as was usual in those days) and beguiled and led Israel astray; that he mocked at the words of the Wise; that he expounded scripture in the same manner as the Pharisees; that he had five disciples; that he said he was not come to take ought away from the Law, or to add to it; that he was hanged (crucified) as a false teacher and beguiler on the eve of the Passover which happened on the Sabbath; and that his disciples healed the sick in his name."

Dr. Klausner gives examples of the Jewish tales. One of them is a bit dirty, and at the same time stupid, so there is no sense in repeating it; it is important only because the teller is known to have belonged to the generation after Jesus, and he states that the tale was told to him by one of the followers of the executed prophet. So good an authority as Klausner takes this as one more bit of evidence that Jesus was an historical person. It is one more clue, to be put with a score of others.

36

Of much greater significance is the testimony of Josephus, the Jewish historian, about whom we have now to hear. He was born shortly after the crucifixion, and was a timeserver and sycophant. First he sympathized with a revolt of the Jews, which came in his early maturity, and he gave the rebels help; but when he saw how things were going, he went over to the other side and pretended that he had been spying upon his own people. He made friends with the Romans and rose rapidly, gained the influence of the Emperor, married a rich wife, and, in short, made a great success of his life from the worldly point of view.

There have been thousands like him through the ages, and we should never have heard his name had it not been that he took up the idea of collecting information and studying the documents of the two centuries preceding his time, and composing a history thereof. He published two volumes, the first called *The Jewish War* and the second *Jewish Antiquities*. He is the only historian of that period and place, and for that reason his books had an enormous success. His works were translated into most of the languages of the then-known world, and have survived through the ages in innumerable editions. An Austrian-Jewish scholar named Robert Eisler specialized in the study of these texts, and in a book called *The Messiah Jesus* he tells in detail the curious story of a famous paragraph known as the *Testimonium of Josephus*.

This sycophant to the Roman rulers of course hated Jesus; he hated all rebels, and Jewish rebels especially, because they brought the Jews into disfavor with the Romans, and at the same time were casting contempt on those Jews who had risen in the Roman service. But in the eighteenth book of his *Jewish Antiquities* Josephus has been made to speak in ardent praise of Jesus, saying flatly that "he was the Christ." For eleven centuries this so-called *Testimonium* was accepted without question by the literate world. The early Church father Eusebius quoted it three times and called it "precious testimony." Coming down through the centuries, we find an old Viennese court librarian calling it "this most precious and estimable jewel."

Eisler says: "The obviously paradoxical fact that an unbelieving Jew should have acknowledged Jesus to have been the true Christ foretold by the prophets was attributed to the peculiar and miraculous power of the Redeemer, which had forced as it were even a recalcitrant infidel to yield to its spell and extracted a blessing from this second Balaam who must have set out to curse. The important fact that he did not himself believe in Jesus as the Christ did not impair the value of his testimony in the eyes of the Church. On the contrary, it was strengthened by the fact that even an unbeliever and an adversary of the faith had reluctantly confessed to its truth. 'And therein the eternal power of Jesus Christ was manifested, that the princes of the synagogue, who had handed him over to death, acknowledged him to be God'; these are the words of Isaac, a converted Jew, writing about 370, and known to the Christians under the name of Gaudentius or Hilarius."

This *Testimonium* was the most obvious of frauds, but it wasn't until the sixteenth century that a scholar found courage to question it, and then a generation later, another scholar found courage to print the questioning. Today no thinking man would defend it; and it has had a curious effect upon present-day scholarship: a group of critics, having rejected the fraud, have decided that Josephus did not mention Jesus at all, and that this is an important piece of evidence to prove that such a man never existed. They argue that a writer who had come in the generation immediately after him, and who had gone into such detail as a historian, could not possibly have failed to mention the crucifixion of a Galilean rebel, and the beginning of a movement to hail him as the Messiah, even as God.

The full text of the *Testimonium* is as follows: "Now about this time there arose Jesus, a wise man, if indeed he may be called a man. For he was a doer of marvelous acts, a teacher of such men as received the truth with delight. And he won over to himself many Jews and many also of the Greek nation. He was the Christ. And when, on the indictment of the principal men among us, Pilate had sentenced him to the cross, still those who before had loved him did not cease to do so. For he appeared to them on the third day alive again, as the divinely inspired prophets had told—these and ten thousand other wonderful things—concerning him. And until now the race of Christians, so named from him, is not extinct."

Eisler from his intimate knowledge of Josephus' mind and style argues that this document had not been made up out of nothing, but represents a modification of an actual statement about Jesus which Josephus had made, and which the Christian editors revised. Consider, for example, the phrase "if indeed he may be called a man." It seems clearly to call for some kind of uncomplimentary remark about Jesus, either preceding it or following it: something to the effect that he was ugly, that he was evil, or that he was a teacher of tricks. The flat statement that he was the Christ might easily have been made out of some sentence to the effect that "he was regarded by many of the Jews as the Christ." The statement that "he appeared on the third day alive again" would easily have been "they believed that, etc." The books of Josephus were written in Greek. The Greek word for 'wise man' is *sophos,* and the Greek word for a betrayer of the truth is *sophistes,* a sophist. How simple for any scribe to make that change! The earliest manuscript of Josephus known to the Western world dates from the eleventh century, so you can see that the interpolators had a thousand years in which to work on one of their heroes. He had become that because of the *Testimonium,* that "precious jewel."

37

In this book I have portrayed Jesus as a desert man, a Rechabite carpenter, small in size and unattractive features. My authority for this is Robert Eisler, and I have accepted him for the reason that, of the many scholars whose works I have read, he impresses me as the most learned and the most open-minded. Some thirty years ago he sent me a set of proofs of the English edition of *The Messiah Jesus,* and the opinion I formed then has lasted ever since. On page 322 of this book he speaks of "the well-attested fact" that Jesus belonged to the class of carpenters, those Cainite or Rechabite 'wayfaring people' from the 'valley of the carpenters.'" He cites ancient Jewish authorities to show that there were men of noble birth, sons of David, among these fugitives, and he shows that among the ancestors of Jesus listed in *Luke 3:37* were Rechabites and Cainites named in *Genesis,* one name meaning the 'smith' (carpenter), another the 'circumciser for God,' and another the 'man who has come down in the world.'

Dr. Eisler goes on to show the extraordinary resemblances between the teachings and practices of Jesus and those of the Rechabites, even down to the Sleb, their descendants of the present day, shown in the frontispiece to his book. You will note by the size of the muskets they hold that they are very small men. They use the muskets only for hunting; as late as 1882 they were reported as using bows and arrows.

The reader is, of course, free to reject my fictional story of the early life of Jesus, but let him not deceive himself with some other man's guess presented as fact. We have no knowledge whatever on the subject. The story of his birth has the obvious features of legend. The story of his parents' fleeing to save him from Herod is in conflict with well-known facts of history. The story of his session with the learned men of the Temple is charming, and may well be true, so I have made use of it. After that the story is a complete blank until his appearance as a public figure, at an age variously guessed at from twenty-five to fifty.

38

Next comes the question, what did Jesus look like? First, we have the Church traditions, and the problem of how much weight we shall give to them. A believing friend of mine points out that I reject many such traditions, and therefore have no right to accept them in the present case. My answer is that traditions which favor the spread of a sacred cause may be regarded with suspicion, but those which go against it must surely have a weight of authority to enable them to survive through the ages. Every scribe who copied a manuscript would be made happy to write that the founder of his faith was god-like in appearance; the same scribe would be in anguish as he wrote that the godly one was small and unprepossessing, and had a crooked back. And yet, such are the traditions which have come down to us.

St. Justin Martyr, Church father of the second century, said as follows, "He appeared without comeliness, as the Scriptures declared." These last words are of major importance to us, for the Scriptures we possess declare nothing of the sort. There is one hint in the New Testament as to his appearance, which I shall mention presently, but there is no clear declaration on the subject; this seems to make certain that the Scriptures we have today differ in that important respect from those known to Justin Martyr. It can only be that the pious scribes cut out the unpleasant descriptions of their revered founder. If they had been pleasant descriptions, they surely would have been allowed to stand.

Clement of Alexandria, another Church Father wrote, "The Lord himself was uncomely in aspect . . . His form was mean, inferior to men." There was a debate on the subject between Origen and Celsus, and the latter argued that it could not be correct to believe that "he was, as they report, little and ill-conditioned and ignoble, i.e. low and mean." Tertullian, mastermind of the early Church who fought in vain against its increasing worldliness, declares that "No matter how poor and despised that body might be, Jesus is still my Christ." In his *Flesh of Christ*, Chapter 9, he says, "His body did not reach even to human beauty, to say nothing of heavenly glory." St. Augustine evidently knew these reports concerning the physical appearance of Jesus, for he says in his work, *De Trinitate*: "Whatever the bodily appearance or face of our Lord was, it was but one, yet it was represented and diversified by a variety of numberless ideals." That is presumably an illustration of what St. Gregory of Nazianzen had in mind when he wrote to St. Jerome that "Nothing can impose better upon the people than verbiage; the less they understand, the more they admire."

Such were the traditions concerning Jesus in the western half of the Christian world. Now let us go to the eastern half and see what we find there. St. Andrew, bishop of Crete at the beginning of the eighth century, wrote as follows: "But moreover the Jew Josephus in like manner narrates that the Lord was seen having connate eyebrows, goodly eyes, long-faced, crooked, well-grown." The word crooked is that Greek word *epíkuphos* which I quoted previously, and it means hunchbacked. Practically the same words are found in a scholion to John of Damascus in two manuscripts in the Bibliothèque Nationale in Paris. Both of these are highly regarded Church Fathers, and surely they did not write such words lightly.

In various Syrian documents edited by Dr. Rendel Harris we find Ephrem Syrus, of the fourth century, writing, "God took human form and appeared in a form of three human ells; he came down to us small of stature." The ell varies, but approximates eighteen inches, which would make a man of four and a half feet, about the height of the modern Sleb, the descendants of the Rechabites. Another treatise of Ephrem, in Armenian, reports, "Our Lord came, he appeared to us as a man small of stature." In the Syriac language is a hymn by Theodore of Mopsuhestia, saying, "Thy appearance, O Christ, was smaller than that of the children of Jacob." Similar testimony is found in the Syrian *Acts of Thomas*. And St. Andrew of Crete makes the same statement as to the mother of Jesus —that she too was small.

39

Most interesting in connection with this problem of the physical appearance of Jesus is Eisler's study of the so-called *Letter of Lentulus,* purporting to have been written by a Roman official in the time of Jesus, but which all scholars now recognize as a Christian forgery. It dates from the latter part of the first century, and was apparently composed by some devout person who was offended by what Josephus had written about the founder of the new faith. The letter shows traces of the Josephus *Testimonium,* and this, of course, was a 'giveaway,' revealing the fact that the letter was of later origin than it purported to be. In later versions these passages were left out.

It is interesting to compare the admiring praises in this Letter with texts of Josephus found in old Slavic and Byzantine manuscripts. During the present century there have been discovered many such manuscripts in monasteries in Poland, Russia, Lithuania, Rumania, and other countries of the Greek Church, the so-called Jewish libraries; for the Jews read Josephus. Also, there were Christian sects in Russia which had started a movement back toward Judaism; that is to say, they became Unitarians, and therefore heretics to the Orthodox Church. At risks of their lives these groups had retained their Josephus.

Many of the Slavic texts were edited and published in the German language by Dr. Alexander Berendts, Leipzig, 1906. These texts were neglected by the scholarly world, and it is Robert Eisler who is credited with having recognized their crucial worth. From them we learn for the first time what Josephus really said about Jesus, and what the censors of the Western churches tried to destroy forever. Thus where Lentulus makes Jesus 'of stature tall,' Josephus reports him as *epíkuphos,* hunchbacked, and only four and a half feet high. Where Lentulus makes him 'beautiful by a ruddy color,' Josephus makes him 'dark.' Where Lentulus makes his hair 'of the color of unripe hazel nuts,' Josephus makes it 'scanty.' Needless to say, it was the Lentulus version which the painters through the centuries have made into the standard 'Jesus'; painting him to the order of prelates and rulers who had the money to pay for works of art.

To conclude this subject, there is the hint in the New Testament, from the lips of Jesus himself. In the fourth chapter of Luke is narrated: "And he came to Nazareth, where he had been brought up: and as his custom was, he went into the synagogue on the Sabbath day, and stood up for to read. And there was delivered unto him the book of the prophet Esaias. And when he had opened the book he found the place where it was written, 'The Spirit of the Lord is upon me, because he hath anointed me to preach the gospel to the poor; he hath sent me to heal the brokenhearted, to preach deliverance to the captives, and recovering of sight to the blind, to set at liberty them that are bruised, to preach the acceptable year of the Lord.' And he closed the book, and he gave it again to the minister, and sat down. And the eyes of all them that were in the synagogue were fastened on him. And he began to say unto them, 'This day is this scripture fulfilled in your ears.' And all bare him witness, and wondered at the gracious words which proceeded out of his mouth. And they said, 'Is not this Joseph's son?' and he said unto them, 'Ye will surely say unto me this proverb, "Physician, heal thyself: whatsoever we have heard done in Capernaum, do also here in thy country." ' And he said, 'Verily I say unto you, No prophet is accepted in his own country.' " (LUKE 4:16–24)

The important detail in this anecdote is the word 'surely,' in connection with the proverb, 'Physician heal thyself.' What can be the meaning of the word, except that there was something physically wrong with Jesus? His manner must have been taunting, for the story continues: "And all they in the synagogue, when they heard these things, were filled with wrath, and rose up, and thrust him out of the city, and led him unto the brow of the hill whereon their city was built, that they might cast him down headlong." (LUKE 4:28–29)

My 'believing friend' cannot understand why I bring in these details about the physical Jesus. He feels that I am trying to 'belittle' a great soul; but as I see it, I am trying to exalt him. The aristocracy, the great ones of the earth through the centuries, have taken him over, making him one like themselves. But Jesus said: "Whosoever exalteth himself shall be abased; and he that humbleth himself shall be exalted." Jesus was a man of the people, who gave offense by eating with publicans and sinners; he was a desert man, who had not where to lay his head. Concerning John the Baptist he asked: "But what went ye out for to see? A man clothed in soft raiment? Behold, they which are gorgeously appareled, and live delicately, are in king's courts."

I think that this man would be content to be himself, and require no prettifying in any book.

40

Josephus also wrote about John the Baptist, and his texts on that subject were not so mutilated by the Christian censors, for the reason that Josephus was interested in the Baptist and did not consider him a menace. I quote from Eisler's book one of those Slavonic Josephus fragments, this one found in Rumania, and designated as *Codex Gaster #89, saec. XVI–XVIII*. It is a fragment called *Story of Joseph Matathie on John:* Matathie being the evangelist Matthew, and John being the Baptist. This is what Josephus narrates:

"About that time, so he told, there was a man going about among the Jews who wore an odd dress. He had pasted the hair of animals on his body wherever it was not covered with his own natural hair; his face looked savage. In his appearance he looked like a ghost rather than a human being, so peculiar it was. He also led a very curious mode of life. He ate no bread, and not even on the Passover did he touch of the unleavened bread, saying that this was meant to remind us of the God who relieved us from bondage. He did not allow wine or other strong drink to come near him. He detested all flesh of animals and abhorred all injustices. He lived only on the buds of trees. He came to the Jews and taught them thus: 'God hath sent me to show you the new path by which you may be freed from many tyrants, so that even death will not have any power over you, but only the Lord above.' When hearing these words, the people followed him; but all he did to them was to plunge them into the water of the Jordan and to tell them to avoid all evil thenceforth. Yet the Pharisees prohibited him from going on with his teaching and from addressing the masses. However, he replied to them: 'You had better give up your evil deeds.' Simeon, the scribe, who was an Essene, rose and said: 'We study the divine laws day after day, whilst thou, like unto a wild animal, hast come forth from the woods, and yet

thou darest to teach us? Thou seducest the people with thy
impure teaching.' And they wanted to rush upon him like
wild animals to kill him. Yet he went over to the other side
of the Jordan and continued his teaching."

41

Yet another Josephus story, even more curious: Under the
reign of the Emperor Maximinus Daia in the year 311, the
Christians were making progress in Rome and were being bit-
terly fought. One of the propaganda acts of this emperor
was to publish to the world the account of the crucifixion of
Jesus which had been sent in by Pontius Pilate, the procurator
of Judea, just after the event. The Roman government was
most careful in its preservation of records, and scholars
admit it is inconceivable that Pilate would have executed a
free man in Jerusalem and failed to turn in the customary
report. Such reports were known as *acta;* and Maximinus
Daia broadcast throughout Rome the text of the particular
actum pilati which had to do with Jesus Christ and why
Pilate had washed his hands of him.

Of course Pilate's account was from the Roman point of
view; and from the point of view of the Christians it was
blasphemy. There was an uproar, and the Christian Bishop
Eusebius, Church Father and historian most highly regarded,
published an answer, arguing that the document was a fraud,
because of the date, given as the year 21 A.D., whereas all the
Christian traditions asserted the crucifixion to have been
about the year 30. A few years later, when the power of sup-
pression came into the hands of the Christians, this so-called
blasphemy was hunted out and destroyed, and no copy of it
has come down to us.

Needless to say, scholars would give much to have this *Act
of Pilate;* and now come these old Slavonic texts of Josephus, dating from the sixteenth century, and among them is a
work entitled in Greek *Halosis,* meaning Honquest—that is,
the conquest of Jerusalem, which took place in 70 A.D. under
the Jewish historian's own eyes. This work contains a de-
tailed account of the crucifixion of Jesus, and Eisler advances
the fascinating theory that Josephus must have had access
to that "Act of Pilate" concerning the case. He could surely
have got it, for he lived in Rome and was a favorite of the
Emperor Titus. Of course the Josephus version had been
doctored by Christian copyists; Eisler indicates such words
as he believes to be interpolations; "he was the only born Son

of God," and such expressions as "god-manlike" and "divine" were surely not written by an anti-Christian Jew.

Earlier in this book you have read the Christian tradition concerning the trial and death of Jesus; now you may witness the same events through the eyes of the opposition. The restored text tells the story of Pilate and the episode of the standards already referred to, and then the story goes on as follows:

"At that time, too, there appeared a certain man of magical power, if it is permissible to call him a man, whom certain Greeks call a son of God, but his disciples the true prophet, said to raise the dead and heal all diseases. His nature and his form were human; a man of simple appearance, mature age, small stature, three cubits high, hunchbacked, with a long face, long nose, and meeting eyebrows, so that they who see him might be affrighted, with scanty hair but with a parting in the middle of his head, after the manner of the Nazirites, and with an undeveloped beard. Only in semblance was he superhuman, for he gave some astonishing and spectacular exhibitions. But again, if I look at his commonplace physique I for one cannot call him an angel. And everything whatsoever he wrought through some invisible power, he wrought through some word and a command. Some said of him, 'Our first lawgiver is risen again and displays many healings and magic arts,' others that 'he is sent from God.' Howbeit in many things he disobeyed the law and kept not the Sabbath according to our fathers' custom. Yet he himself did nothing shameful or high-handed, but by his word he prepared everything.

"And many of the multitude followed after him and accepted his teaching, and many souls were excited, thinking that thereby the Jewish tribes might be freed from Roman hands. But it was his custom most of the time to abide over against the city on the Mount of Olives, and there too he bestowed his healings upon the people. And there assembled unto him of helpers one hundred and fifty and a multitude of the mob.

"Now when they saw his power, how that he accomplished whatsoever he would by a magic word, and when they had made known to him their will, that he should enter into the city, cut down the Roman troops and Pilate and rule over us, he disdained us not. And having all flocked into Jerusalem, they raised an uproar against Pilate, uttering blasphemies alike against God and against Caesar.

"And when therefore knowledge of it came to the Jewish leaders, they assembled together with the high priest and spake: 'We are powerless and too weak to withstand the Romans. But seeing that the bow is bent we will go and impart to Pilate what we have heard, and we shall be safe, lest he hear of it from others and we be robbed of our substance and ourselves slaughtered and the children of Israel dispersed.'

"And they went and imparted the matter to Pilate, and he sent and had many of the multitude slain. And he had that wonder-worker brought up, and instituting an enquiry concerning him, he passed this sentence upon him: 'He is a malefactor, a rebel, a robber thirsting for the crown.' And they took him and crucified him according to the custom of their fathers."

Such appears to be the true *Testimonium* of Josephus. The phrase 'the bow is bent' is a reference to *Psalm 11*, "For lo, the wicked bend their bow, they make ready their arrow upon the string, that they may privily shoot at the upright in heart." Such a reference would be understood only by Jews, and is one more indication that the text was written by a Jew.

42

As to the date of the crucifixion given in the document of Maximinus Daia: A.D. 21, Eisler believes that it is the correct date, following upon the disturbance over the raising of the standards on the Temple hill, A.D. 19. For the purpose of this book it is sufficient to repeat the fact that no one knows positively any exact date concerning Jesus. The Christians make him about thirty when he died; Josephus in the Slavic version makes him about fifty. Hastings Hictionary of the Bible gives the date of his birth at B.C. 7–6; the *Enclyopedia Biblica* of Berlin gives the birth as about 4 B.C. If we take the earlier date and combine it with the Roman date of 21 for the crucifixion, we have Jesus twenty-eight at that time. It is hard to see how the Romans would have found advantage in inventing a false date for the event. That Jesus should have set out on his mission as a result of the excitement over the setting up of the standards on the Temple hill seems to offer the best explanation of his sudden emergence into public life. Thousands were aroused, and he was one of them.

As to the question of the month, and the day of the month in which he was born, and the month and the day of the month on which he died 'and rose again,' all that needs to be said is, that both Easter and Christmas are the oldest dates in the world; they were celebrated in all the religions of antiquity. The Christmas season is the time of the winter solstice, when the sun god, having almost disappeared in the sky, begins to come back to bless mankind. As for the Easter festival, that is the vernal equinox, the springtime, when fertility rites are called for to continue the cycle of life. It is amusing to note that for three hundred years the Christians celebrated Easter as the birthdate of their founder, and only shifted to the winter solstice in 345 A.D. by decree of Pope Julian II, who was disturbed by the fact that Jesus was honored at the same time as Mithras and Bacchus.

That we have taken over the fertility rites of the ancient religions with their Easter eggs and bunnies seems harmless enough; but our Santa Claus has been corrupted by commercialism, and Christmas has become a festival of department stores and newspapers which print their advertising. It is the same thing which happened to the Jews, when a simple pastoral people built a great city and turned their Temple into a livestock exchange. If Jesus came back to earth today, he would have to drive the moneychangers out for a second time; he wouldn't be crucified for it, but would surely be locked up, and what the newspapers would say about him would not be full of loving-kindness.

As for the priests and Pharisees who shouted for his death, they now operate a world-wide Church machine in his name. The age-old deity has become, in the words of the Scottish poet, Robert Buchanan:

> Great Christus-Jingo, at whose feet
> Christian and Jew and Atheist meet.

A believer in prophecy might claim the word Atheist in the above lines as an inspiration from on high: this since the disciples of Lenin have chosen their role as the newest world conquerors. The poet continues:

> O gentle Jew, from age to age
>   Walking the waves thou could'st not tame,
> This god hath ta'en thy heritage,
>   And stolen thy sweet and stainless Name!
> To him we crawl and bend the knee,
> Naming thy Name, but scorning Thee!

43

When the Christians were outlaws hiding in catacombs, their ability to doctor manuscripts was for the most part limited to their own. Each sect would take out whatever material was not in accordance with its notions and put in new material to their taste. But later on, when they came into power, they were in possession not merely of their own manuscripts but of all the treasures of antiquity up to that time; they then immediately began a furious war upon everything in these writings which did not accord with their doctrines, and they imposed a death penalty for the keeping of proscribed books.

On this subject I could write a whole volume, and many such volumes have been written. A Christian mob burned the great library of Alexandria. St. Gregory burned the Imperial library of the Apollo. Twenty-four volumes of the works of the gnostic philosopher Basilides were burned by the order of the Church, so we are told by Eusebius. The pre-Christian Gaelic civilizations of Britain, Ireland, and Brittany were wiped out with all their literary treasures. Kuhn tells us that "a Christian mob destroyed the city of Bibractis in 389 in Gaul, and Alesia was destroyed before that. Bibractis had a sacred college of the Druids with forty thousand students, giving courses in philosophy, literature, grammar, jurisprudence, medicine, astrology, architecture, and esoteric religion. Arles, founded two thousand years before Christ, was sacked in 270 A.D."

The crusaders destroyed all Jewish manuscripts and books in the path of their invasions, and similar destructive work was carried on by the Inquisitions both in France and Spain. Cardinal Ximenes "delivered to the flames in the square of Granada eighty thousand Arabic manuscripts, among them translations of the classical authors." Thirty-six volumes written by Porphyry were destroyed by the early Church fathers. These and thousands of similar episodes great and small account for the fact that ancient manuscripts are so rare, and that we have to piece together out of fragments of writing our information concerning the civilizations of the past.

As soon as Christianity had won its struggle for power, the properly saved began to hunt down the heretics—in the name of a Savior who had told them that the first great commandment was to love the Lord thy God, and that the second was like unto it, to love thy neighbor as thyself. The Holy Church evolved a technique of evasion; it would not itself do any harm to anybody, but would find the heretic guilty and then turn him over to what was called 'the secular arm' to be duly and properly burned at the stake. It so happened that the technique was identical with that which was used against Jesus himself; the chief priest and the other churchly ones found him guilty, and then turned him over to Pilate to be sentenced and executed. Thus the pious ones stand innocent before the bar of history.

These proceedings went on through the centuries. They make painful reading, and naturally many devout persons would prefer that they were not read. But the theme of this book is not merely the spirit of Jesus, but what men have done with it. The story of Christianity is one, not merely of divine love and heroic saints and martyrs; it is a story of fanaticism and dreadful cruelty. Eight military crusades were conducted in an effort to redeem the imaginary tomb of Christ from the Saracens. There was even a Children's Crusade, when tens of thousands of helpless bewildered innocents wandered off to their death. What did it matter, so long as their souls were saved and they were taken up into heaven? A truly unforeseen consequence of a belief in immortality!

Such was the formula by which Torquemada as head of the Spanish Inquisition justified all the horrors he perpetrated. It was better that a hundred innocent souls should be sent to heaven than that a single emissary of Satan should be left on earth to destroy souls by the spreading of heretical doctrines. In my student days I read Lea's *History of the Inquisition of the Middle Ages* and his *History of the Inquisition in Spain*, and their effect has never been forgotten. I read the story of the horrors of the St. Bartholomew massacres in France, in which fifty thousand Protestants were slaughtered. Large sections of the population of France, the most intelligent and industrious, were exterminated wholesale, first the Albigenses and then the Huguenots. This remained the most awful record in history until the days of Hitler and Stalin.

There was no country without its martyrs. Latimer and Cranmer were burned in England; John Huss was burned in Bohemia; Savonarola and Giordano Bruno were burned in Italy. Galileo was imprisoned in a dungeon because he dared to say that the earth went round the sun. The doctors of the Church did not have time to look through his telescope; they were too busy killing people who refused to believe in the

Trinity. Roger Williams was driven into exile among savages, and poor old women were hanged as witches in Massachusetts. And if you think that all this is old-time history, I point out that Franco in Spain has been shooting Socialists, Democrats, Liberals, Freemasons, and Protestants for the past fifteen years.

44

It was in the year 337 A.D. that the Emperor Constantine became a convert on his deathbed, and before the end of the fourth century Christianity had become the official religion of the Roman state. Its doctrines were laid down by a Church Council which met at Nicea in 325, and from that we have the so-called Nicene Creed. All this had been achieved in a little more than three hundred years since the crucifixion. It was a triumph for the Church, and for its founder a temporary defeat. It meant that his enemies had taken over his name, his teachings, and his influence.

By 'enemies' I don't mean the Jews, who were a small group and comparatively unimportant; I mean the great Roman Empire, which had stood in the background of his life and with callous cruelty had inflicted death upon him. The Rechabite carpenter had said, "You cannot serve God and mammon," and to him the great Roman Empire must have been the incarnation of mammon; it was power worship, money worship, the glorification of material things. Now the priests who operated in his name would design for themselves elaborate costumes covered with gold and jewels. They would erect magnificent temples, ostensibly to his glory, but really to their own. They would become 'princes of the Church,' and would control the souls of men, and teach them folly and nonsense, and repress all intellectual progress. They would hold the terrors of hell over the people; they would sell forgiveness of sins for money, and spend that money to buy lands and increase their grip upon worldly affairs. They would persecute heretics and burn thousands at the stake. Gerald Massey estimates that during the Christian era no fewer than two million persons gave their lives in the struggle for intellectual freedom in Europe. And all this cruelty and tyranny in the name of a humble carpenter who had no place to lay his head, and who had taught his followers "The kingdom of God is within you."

It is my belief that these evils developed in the Catholic Church, because it teaches fixed dogmas, and interposes its

authority between man and his Creator. In so saying I am
speaking of the Church machine; I do not include the humble
followers, most of whom live hard-working lives and do the
best they know; nor do I include the rank and file of the
priests and nuns, who obey their superiors blindly, and work
faithfully at trying to remedy the miseries they see about
them. Worldly power is the thing that Jesus hated and denounced, and worldly power is what the Church hierarchy
has held and used in the support of bigotry and reaction. If
Jesus has indeed been sitting at the right hand of his Father
and watching it, he must have sweated tears of blood as he
did in Gethsemane.

45

For a dozen centuries this 'Holy Catholic Church,' which
calls Peter its first pope, ruled the mind of Europe practically
without challenge; but then came a new and strange development in the western part of the continent. The quarrel between Peter and Paul, so long repressed, flamed up anew;
Paul's spirit forged to the front and took charge of a second
birth of Christianity. The power of the Pope was overthrown
in the German and English lands; the Bible was translated
into the living languages, and the common man reasserted the
right to save his own soul in his own way.

There are few events in human history more dramatic than
this resurgence of Paul after sixteen hundred years of sup-
pression. No Catholic will agree, but I think it correct to say
that most progress which the Western world has made in
freedom and enlightenment has been due to that transformation. It is the Protestant lands which have democracy and
science, while the lands over which Peter still rules have over-
population, poverty and superstition. Spain is the perfect
example of such a land; while in Ireland you see the spirits of
Peter and Paul making faces at each other over a border, and
hardly to be kept from flying at each other's throats.

Not that I mean to glorify the Pauline theology, which has
spawned vast hordes of bigots. It was the Protestant John
Calvin who contributed to the burning of his rival, Servetus,
in Switzerland; and Protestantism proceeded to split into
hundreds of different sects. Every man who read Paul's
preachments felt free to decide what he meant, and to gather
a group of people who called themselves the only true believers. The end product has been numerous groups of devoted and self-sacrificing persons, and other groups of pathetic

and deluded bigots. In Southern California, where I am writing this book, I hear over the radio fanatics screaming about the blood of Jesus Christ, the Lamb of God, and threatening sinners with hell fire. They work themselves into a frenzy; you hear them gasping for breath, and you think that the next moment they must fall to the floor in convulsions.

I turn the dial quickly; but there are thousands who listen, and send in money to pay for such broadcasts. The same thing is going on in thousands of small churches scattered over our South and West. It is called "Fundamentalism," and its slogan is "The old-time religion! It was good for my fathers and it's good enough for me." It has managed to forbid by law the teaching of evolution in the schools of Tennessee, and its devotees are the natural prey of reactionary demagogs. It bases itself upon a Holy Book whose texts are hopelessly corrupted, and it is as alien to the free spirit of Jesus as Catholicism with its heavenly hierarchy and its worship of images and bones.

This is, of course, only one side of the story of the Christian Church. I am well aware that there is another side; that there have been, and are today, millions of devoted and heroic souls who have absorbed the true spirit of Jesus, and who labor to the best of their understanding to live according to his teachings. These millions have been and are the mainstays of our civilization, and without them it might speedily decay. The effort of this book is not to destroy their faith in Jesus; the effort is to transfer their faith from Jesus to that Heavenly Father whom Jesus loved. This transfer is something which no one need fear—any more than Jesus feared it, when he set aside the dogmas and delusions of the Jewish faith which had been taught to him in his childhood, and which had doubtless seemed wondrous and holy to him until his mind matured.

46

Yet Jesus lives. . . . Men read his inspiring words, they make note of his selfless life and his pitiful death. The idea of a God of love becomes real to them, and it kindles a fire in their souls. They are moved to follow his example, and all over the world the struggle against entrenched evil goes on. It goes on inside the churches, to bring them into accord with his plain and simple teachings. It goes on outside the churches, with men who have learned to do as Jesus did, to pray in secret and tell no man about it. It goes on in the hearts of those who call themselves agnostics, even those who call themselves atheists—for they battle in the name of truth, and their battle is a part of the working of the spirit. "By their fruits ye shall know them," Jesus said; and if a man has a field full of weeds he has to plow them up before he can plant the good seed. The superstitions and follies which the churches believe and teach are surely weeds, and bring the very idea of religion into disrepute among thinking people.

I say that Jesus lives. His spirit works in men and women all over the world. It moves them to seek for truth, and to speak it when they have found it. Some stay in the churches and struggle against the corruption and worldliness they meet there. History is full of the records of persons like this, as well as of the missionaries who go out into distant places, carrying the story of Jesus to primitive peoples whose ideas and practices of religion are of a lower order. Read Parkman's *History of the Jesuits in North America*. These volumes, taken from reports sent home by the missionaries who came from France to what is now Canada and the northern part of the United States, tell moving stories of men who endured tortures and indignities from ferocious savages. They continued in the spirit of love, preaching the gospel of the crucified teacher of love; in the end love conquered, and the Six Nations and other Indian tribes accepted the Christian creed. Of course the traders came in with their rum, smallpox, and syphilis, and over these the Jesuits had no control.

The same thing is going on today in all the backward parts of the world. Missionaries, both Protestant and Catholic, are carrying modern medicine and hygiene to primitive peoples, and devoting their lives to such service. Albert Schweitzer comes to mind, not merely because he has had much publicity, but because of his book, *The Quest of the Historical Jesus,* a work of impressive learning. If you want to know what two generations of German scholars have established by their textual study of the New Testament, you can find it in this book. Schweitzer, musician, scientist, and medical man, became seized by the spirit of the Jesus whom he had studied; he dropped his connections with the civilized world and went away into the jungles of Africa to bring medical help to suffering natives. What he believes about Jesus would not satisfy either Catholic or Fundamentalist but very certainly it would have satisfied Jesus.

47

Modern science has been busy upon our physical universe
and its complicated problems. As a student in a physics class
at college, at the age of fourteen, I had a learned German in-
structor with a black beard. I recall as well as if it were yes-
terday a scene in the laboratory, when one of the students
said to him, "But, Professor, suppose they should some day
split the atom?" The reply was prompt and positive, "Oh,
they can never do that!"

The year was 1892 or 1893, and Roentgen was on the
verge of discovering X-rays and Becquerel of discovering
radioactivity. It wasn't many years before the atom was split;
now there are electrons, protons, deuterons, neutrons, posi-
trons, neutrinos, photons, several kinds of mesons—and I
learn in my morning paper that at Berkeley they have discovered a couple more to which they have not yet given
names. The universe is no longer a lot of little hard lumps
whose permanence we can count upon. Each little lump is
a universe in itself, mostly empty space with unimaginably
minute particles whirling round a central nucleus, exactly
as our planets behave about the sun. And the 'particles' are
not lumps, they are energy. Sir James Jeans tells us that the
best picture we can now form of the universe is of a soap
bubble with wrinkles on its skin. The wrinkles are waves and
that is all there is left of matter; the eminent English physicist
tells us that the waves are just as apt to be mental as physical. He says: "The universe can best be pictured . . . as con-
sisting of pure thought, the thought of what, for want of a
wider word, we must describe as a mathematical thinker."

All I can add about this is that when the time comes that
governments are ready to spend as much money upon research in the human mind as they have spent upon the building of A-bombs and H-bombs, then possibly we may make
discoveries about what the subconscious mind is, and how
it works, and what we can do with it. Then we may be really
in a position to explain 'miracles' and to work them. Then
we shall really know that the world is one, and shall understand the truth of Tennyson's lines:

> Flower in the crannied wall,
> I pluck you out of the crannies,
> I hold you here, root and all, in my hand,
> Little flower—but *if* I could understand

What you are, root and all, and all in all
I should know what God and man is.

Jesus would have understood those lines: He knew that he had in himself a wellspring of love, of joy and hope and aspiration, which is what distinguishes men from the animals. He knew that by fasting and prayer that wellspring could be caused to flow more freely from its source. He had a name for the source; he called it his heavenly Father. God was and is the Creator, and the living Presence in every man and woman. He is a God of love, and because He loves men, men must love Him; because all men are children of a loving Father, all men must love one another. These are the two moral laws according to Jesus, and concerning them there can be no compromise. "I say unto you, 'Love your enemies, bless them that curse you, do good to them that hate you, and pray for them who despitefully use you, and persecute you; that ye may be the children of your Father which is in heaven.'"

48

Every man can remember crises in his moral life when he made a choice for good or evil. This writer recollects a dinner party in the 1920s where he met a Hungarian who afterwards was revealed to have been the head agent of the Comintern in the United States at that time. He said, "I have read a number of your books, and what impresses me is the sound spirit of *hate* in them." The writer got an inner shock; he went off and thought it over and wondered if that was really what he had put into his books. He had not intended it so; he thought he had been following the Christian maxim, to hate the sin and love the sinner. He made up his mind that from that time on he would strive consciously to put love into his books; to be more constructive and less destructive, and in exposing a social disease always to lay stress upon the remedy.

The writer's wife also recalls a moral experience. At a dinner party she sat next to John Dewey, and expressed to that philosopher the anxiety she was feeling concerning the development of the revolution in Russia, which at the beginning had inspired so much hope in American Socialists. This also was in the '20s, and she remarked, "They are following the maxim that the end justifies the means; and I am afraid of it." Dewey's reply was, "The means *become* the end."

Husband and wife talked it over on the way home, and have talked it over since then, finding it one of the wisest remarks they ever heard. It sums up the whole tragic course of the Russian revolution as we have watched it over a period of thirty-five years. The means were violence and terror, trickery and falsehood; and these means have become the end. I have portrayed the degeneration of Christianity as having taken centuries, but the Russian revolution has degenerated in three decades—so much more rapid is the pace of the world today. The idealists among the old Bolsheviks have been executed; all democratic procedure has been eliminated from both government and industry; the propagandists of the Kremlin have adopted Hitler's maxim, that the bigger the lie the more easy to get it believed; and the expansionist program of victorious Russia has become identical with that of their former Tsars. It is safe to assert that Marx and Engels and Jaurès and Keir Hardie would be as much shocked by the present-day Politburo as Jesus and his disciples would have been shocked by Torquemada and Bloody Mary.

What are we going to do about it? Talk love to the tough masters of the Kremlin? The idea brings a smile; but here we are discussing the spirit of Jesus, and there can be no question that that is what Jesus would require. Instead of heeding him, both sides are busily constructing atomic bombs which are capable of destroying whole cities, and hydrogen bombs which are expected to be a thousand times more deadly than these. Are the Russians going to wipe out New York and Washington, Chicago, Detroit, and Los Angeles— and are we in return going to wipe out Moscow and Leningrad, Kiev, Kharkov, and Vladivostok? If so, it may well mean the end of our present culture, and a return to the way of life of the Rechabites of ancient Transjordan.

49

We are handicapped in our efforts to talk love to the Kremlin for the reason that we ourselves are living a double life, and are torn in half by the conflict in our institutions. In our political affairs we have democracy, with government of the people, by the people, for the people; but in our economic life we have autocracy, and exploitation of the many for the benefit of the few. Here again Jesus has told us in the plainest language that tongue can utter, "No man can serve two masters: for either he will hate the one, and love the other;

or else he will hold to the one, and despise the other. Ye
cannot serve God and mammon."

The early Christians took this literally. They realized the
basic fact that you cannot have love and brotherhood in religious and social life while at the same time you are having
competition and exploitation in economic life. We are told in
Acts: "And all that believed were together, and had all things
common; and sold their possessions and goods, and parted
them to all men, as every man had need. And they continuing
daily with one accord in the Temple, and breaking bread
from house to house, did eat their meat with gladness and
singleness of heart, praising God, and having favour with all
the people." (ACTS 2·44–47)

And then again, "And the multitude of them that believed
were of one heart and of one soul: neither said any of them
that aught of the things which he possessed was his own; but
they had all things common. Neither was there any among
them that lacked: for as many as were possessors of lands or
houses sold them, and brought the prices of the things that
were sold, and laid them down at the apostles' feet: and dis-
tribution was made unto every man according as he had need.
Hand Joses . . . having land, sold it, and brought the money,
and laid it at the apostles' feet." (ACTS 4:32 . . . 34–37)

You will say, of course, that nothing like this could be done
in the modern world. They said the same thing to Jesus in his
time, but it didn't cause him to alter his teachings. Consider
once more the story of the rich young man: "Jesus said unto
him, 'If thou wilt be perfect, go and sell that thou hast, and
give to the poor, and thou shalt have treasure in heaven: and
come and follow me.' But when the young man heard that
saying, he went away sorrowful: for he had great possessions." (MATTHEW 19:21–22)

If we really mean to follow Jesus, what we have to do is to
convert our industry into a public service in which every
worker has a share by right. It does not require any violence,
terror, or deception. Thus we could abolish strikes, unemployment, and crises from our civilization, and confront the rest
of the world as friends, not as exploiters. All that is required
is love, guided by wisdom; and any time we are ready to do
it we can count upon help from the spirit of Jesus. People
would then be able to say that they were really trying to be
Christian, and to use that word without making it a mockery.

In the early days of this century, when we young Socialists
were ardent and hopeful, there was published a poem by

Elizabeth Waddell which all of us loved. I quote it as my
closing words on the Galilean Messiah and his message.

> They have taken the tomb of our Comrade Christ—
>   Infidel hordes that believe not in Man;
> Stable and stall for his birth sufficed,
>   But his tomb is built on a kingly plan.
> They have hedged him round with pomp and parade,
>   They have buried him deep under steel and stone—
> But we come leading the great Crusade
>   To give our Comrade back to his own.

POSTSCRIPT

THE manuscript of this book was read by a scholar of an
orthodox turn of mind, and the author was permitted to
see his opinion. Since the objections he raised may occur to
others, it seems wise to take note of them. The report reads:

"His guesswork would not intrigue his readers particu-
larly; he gives them no guide as to his standard for selecting
and rejecting Biblical material, nor is there anything in what
he says to reassure the skeptical that he has any better access
to the truth than the next man. The skeptic might be encouraged to think that he was writing 'truth' because his views
of many points differ from those which are generally accepted.
But the honest skeptic would require more than this, for there
is a logical fallacy here. Novelty is no more likely to be true
than false; in fact, if the probability lies anywhere, it is on the
side of falsehood.

"The book suffers most from the fact that the uninformed
reader is not able to tell when he is reading Sinclair fiction
and when he is reading factual historical background. Often
the two merge imperceptibly. His history is old stuff, and his
fiction is not new. Many feet have beaten these paths before
his time, and he is following a well-worn route."

The last statement is obviously true. My own feet have been
beating these paths since childhood, and I have only to watch
the book reviews in order to know that new lives and inter-
pretations of Jesus are published frequently. But I am led to
wonder if my critic may not have forgotten the preface of my
book by the time he had read to the end of it. The figures I
quoted from the Gallup poll, revealing that fifty-three per

cent of Americans interviewed could not name one of the Gospel authors, and only thirty-six per cent could name all four of them—these certainly do not seem to indicate that lives of Jesus are superfluous or that quotations from the Gospels are always "old stuff." "Tell me the old old story," runs the Gospel hymn, and I have accepted the invitation.

Not only are books about Jesus published but they are read. My old friend Fulton Oursler, former editor of *Liberty* magazine, recently published one called *The Greatest Story Ever Told.* He became a convert to Catholicism and accepted the doctrines of that Church as God-given. I have seen in the publisher's advertisements the figures as to the astounding circulation of that book; a million copies through the Book of the Month Club, ten million readers in the newspaper serialization, and several times that many million listening to installments over the radio. Against this organ diapason I can raise but a feeble skeptical piping. But having been in opposition to received opinion nearly all my life, I have learned to take the situation calmly. If what I say is true, it will prevail, and if it be not true, I would not wish it to prevail. If the Catholic Church is right I shall burn in hell for all eternity—but I shall believe it only when I feel the flames.

Next, my critic's complaint that I give my readers "no guide as to my standard for selecting and rejecting Biblical material." Again it appears that he has forgotten what he read in the preface to the book. I ask the reader to go back to that preface and note my explanation of the basis upon which I have attempted to sort out truth from falsehood. It is the special business of a novelist to judge human character. By the words, the behavior, the gestures, the accents, the facial expressions of a human being he forms a concept of what is going on in that being's soul. By an extension of the process he conceives an imaginary character, and endeavors to make that character real and understandable to his public by means of the words he puts into the character's mouth, and the descriptions he gives of the character's behavior, gestures, accents, and facial expressions. He becomes a novelist by virtue of his ability to perform this particular feat.

Now the writer has applied this technique to the life and character of Jesus called the Christ. Since early childhood he has been hearing the story, then reading it in several languages; he has been pondering it lovingly, and out of this labor of mind and spirit has formed a conception of what seems to him a living man. He thinks of this man and feels about him as a friend, and ventures to say concerning this friend that he would speak certain words and would not speak certain others; that he would perform certain actions and not others.

Such is the basis upon which this book has been written; such is my "standard for selecting and rejecting Biblical material." I will go farther and say that the scholar to whom I am replying follows the same method and has the same standard, whether he realizes it or not. There can be no other standard for dealing with "Biblical material," for this material is full of contradictions and inconsistencies, and there is nothing you can do but go through it and pick out the things which conform to your own ideas—in most cases those you were taught when you were a child. Every man who reads the Bible makes his own Jesus, and the writing of such a book as this represents an effort on the author's part to provide a Jesus who may be acceptable to modern minds.

To show what I mean: Take your New Testament and begin with the first words: "The book of the generation of Jesus Christ, the Son of David, the Son of Abraham." There follows a long list of Jewish names with the word "begat" between them. You learn that between Jesus and his ancestor Abraham there were forty-two generations; and then you turn to the third chapter of the third Gospel, that according to Luke, and you there find another list of the generations of Jesus and learn that there were fifty-five. I set aside the question as to what any of these ancestors had to do with a man who was not the son of his mother's husband, but the Son of God, conceived by the Holy Ghost. Luke gets us around that difficulty by putting in parentheses the words "as was supposed"; but that does not get us away from the flat contradiction between forty-two and fifty-five ancestors for Joseph the husband of Mary. If you say that this is of no consequence, I answer that the Bible is the Word of God. Why does the Word of God start off with something which is of no consequence, and repels so many readers? I know a lady of a great heart and skeptical mind who decided in her old age that it was her duty to learn about Jesus. She picked up the New Testament and began to read, but was dismayed by what she called "all those begats." She never made another attempt at the Bible, and there are Christians who will say that thereby she lost her immortal soul.

I could continue along this line, setting forth Biblical contradictions and inconsistencies; but this indeed would be 'old

stuff.' Hundreds of such books have been written, beginning
with Voltaire and coming down through Thomas Paine and
Robert Ingersoll to Joseph McCabe and his publisher Halde-
man-Julius. I mention the subject only in order to establish
my thesis, that no man dealing with Biblical material has any
other choice than to go through it and pick out those things
which seem to him to form a consistent and believable picture.

My critic makes the assertion that "novelty is no more
likely to be true than false." He goes on to add that if the
probability lies anywhere it is the novelty that is more apt to
be false. I can only invite my critic to consider the absurdities
which have been believed and promulgated upon the authority
of the Bible and in the name of Jesus. Consider the preposter-
ous notions over which the theologians have wrangled through
the ages, whipping themselves into such a fury that they have
been willing to burn one another at the stake, and indeed have
done so in thousands of cases. It is the Catholics who base
their faith upon Church tradition, and it is to them that we
must go for examples of what this attitude leads to. Take the
latest demonstration, offered to the world while this book is
being written: half a million pilgrims, coming from all corners
of the earth, assemble in Rome and cheer themselves into a
frenzy over the solemn announcement by the Pope that by
revelation from God he declares that the Virgin Mary upon
her death was physically taken up into heaven—'the Assump-
tion,' the doctrine is called.

Consider all the facts which modern science has patiently
gleaned concerning outer space. Consider the changes of
alternating extreme heat and cold through which a body
would have to pass in the ionosphere and other atmospheric
layers. Consider the deadly cold of outer space, precisely absolute zero. Consider the trillions of miles to the nearest
galaxy, and the fiercely glowing temperatures of its millions
of suns, ten thousand or perhaps twenty thousand degrees
of heat. The woman was physically taken to heaven, declared
the Pope, and you must believe it or you are a heretic, and
will go to hell. But where is the hell, and where is the heaven,
among the billions of galactic systems?

If you ask such questions of the true believer he will say
that you are being vulgarly literal. But I ask, is not the vulgar
literalness attributable to those who imagine the physical
body of a woman being subjected to those impossible physical
conditions? The body of a woman has lungs which are intended to breathe air; and what has that body to do in outer

space where there is no trace of air? The body of a woman has warm blood and a heart to pump it; who can imagine blood being pumped under temperatures which would freeze it solid, or would heat it to a point where the trillions of atoms composing it would be converted into electrons flying apart with the speed of light? Is it not obvious that a human body is a product of earth conditions? And what would be the sense of transporting it into a set of conditions to which it has no conceivable relation? It seems to me that Jesus gave his answer to this when he said: "Neither shall they say, Lo here! or, lo there! for, behold, the kingdom of God is within you." (LUKE 17:21)

Officially, there is only one Catholic Jesus; but you may be sure that the Jesus worshiped by the Sicilian peasant woman is different from that of the great prince of the Church who remarked with a sly smile, "In Rome the faith is made; elsewhere it is received." In the same way there are innumerable varieties of Jesus to be found in the Protestant sects, and each is a product of the process of "selecting and rejecting Biblical material." I can hear them arguing in the little Baptist church which has been built next to my home!

While this book was being readied for the printer there appeared in the *New Statesman and Nation* (London) October 27, 1951, an article by C. E. M. Joad entitled *The Twilight of the Church*—meaning, of course, the Church of England. I quote an item of information which was new to me and may be to the reader:

"In 1922 a Commission on Christian Doctrine was set up by the two Archbishops. After fifteen years' deliberation, it published its report in 1938. Those who do not realise how much water has flowed under the clerical bridges during the last fifty years would be surprised to find what opinions may be held and taught without censure by ordained clergymen.

"To mention one or two outstanding examples, the tradition of the verbal inerrancy of the Bible is abandoned. It is no longer necessary to hold that Creation consisted of a series of sudden successive acts; many believe it to be a continuous process. To believe in the existence of Satan and of evil spirits is no longer obligatory; on such matters the language of the Liturgy may be interpreted in 'a purely symbolic sense.' So, too, with the belief in Hell. The belief in Christ's miracles is optional. Many hold that 'It is more congruous with the wisdom and majesty of God that he should never vary the regularities of nature.' The Virgin Birth disappears, leaving the manner of Christ's Incarnation indefinite. So, too, with the physical Ascension into Heaven, of which the Commission report that its physical features are to be interpreted symbolically, since they are closely related to the conception of Heaven as 'a place locally fixed beyond the sky.'"

From this it would appear that I am not alone in claiming the privilege of "selecting and rejecting biblical material." The clergy of the Church of England have the same privilege, officially granted to them. Possibly that may be the reason why I found an English publisher for this book at the first try, but had to make a dozen tries in my own country, and only succeeded when I advertised in the *New Republic* for a publisher who was willing to risk antagonizing "those powerful groups which exist to perpetuate ancient myths." So this book goes out under a heavy handicap.

I was interested to know whether any such action had ever been taken by the Protestant Episcopal Church of America. I made inquiry of Dr. Guy Emery Shipler, long time editor of *The Churchman*, the highly respected organ of the church of my boyhood. He tells me that he knows of no such action having been taken; but he adds: "When I was a seminary student nearly fifty years ago all of the positions outlined by the Commission on Christian Doctrine of England were already acceptable to Episcopal clergymen—except with reservations on one or two points by Anglo-Catholics (High Churchmen)."

My comment on this is that the positions were certainly not acceptable to the Rector of the Church of the Holy Communion in New York, nor to his assistant. I left that church at the age of fifteen or sixteen because I could not accept these very dogmas. Nor do I believe that the positions were acceptable to those New York publishers' readers who advised against the publication of this book on the grounds that it would give offense to too many members of influential church groups. I am led to wonder whether all Episcopal clergymen are being entirely frank with their congregations.

The controversy goes on, and will go on for centuries. All that this writer can do is to urge you to think for yourself and to know what you believe and why. What you believe about Jesus will make a great difference in your own moral life. It is possible to become a great and good man or woman without ever having heard the name of Jesus; but it is much easier if you have learned to know him and love him. His spirit is contagious, and we need it in the dreadful problems which confront us in these years of cold wars alternating with hot.

OTHER BOOKS BY
SYNERGY INTERNATIONAL

Author - Jack London

MARTIN EDEN

WAR OF THE CLASSES

JOHN BARLEYCORN

THE PEOPLE OF THE ABYSS

JACK LONDON ON THE ROAD

THE ASSASSINATION BUREAU, LTD.

THE IRON HEEL

Author – B. Traven

GENERAL FROM THE JUNGLE

THE DEATH SHIP

THE REBELLION OF THE HANGED

THE WHITE ROSE

THE BRIDGE IN THE JUNGLE

MARCH TO THE MONTERIA

THE TREASURE OF THE SIERRA MADRE

Author - Carl Frederick

est PLAYING THE GAME THE NEW WAY

Authors - Frederick Ellis & Carl Frederick

THE OAKLAND STATEMENT

Author – Mao Tsetung

QUOTATIONS FROM CHAIRMAN MAO TSETUNG

Author – Upton Sinclair

OUR LADY

THE FLIVVER KING: THE STORY OF FORD-AMERICA

ONE HUNDRED PERCENT: THE STORY OF A PATRIOT

WORLD'S END I

WORLD'S END II

THE SECRET LIFE OF JESUS

THE MONEYCHANGERS

MENTAL RADIO

THE MILLENNIUM

A PERSONAL JESUS

PROFITS OF RELIGION

THEY CALL ME CARPENTER: A TALE OF
THE SECOND COMING

Author – Thomas Paine

COMMON SENSE, THE RIGHTS OF MAN
& THE AGE OF REASON

THE AMERICAN CRISIS

Author – Karl Marx

DAS KAPITAL

THE COMMUNIST MANIFESTO &
WAGES, PRICE AND PROFIT

WAGE-LABOUR AND CAPITAL
& VALUE. PRICE AND PROFIT

Author – W. E, B. Du Bois

THE SOULS OF BLACK FOLK

Author – Eugene Debs

WALLS AND BARS

Author – Jean-Jacques Rousseau

THE SOCIAL CONTRACT

Author – John Reed

TEN DAYS THAT SHOOK THE WORLD

INSURGENT MEXICO

Author – Antonio Gramsci

THE MODERN PRINCE AND
SELECTED WRITINGS

Author – V. I. Lenin

THE STATE AND REVOLUTION

FIGHT AGAINST STALINISM & IMPERIALISM:
THE HIGHEST STAGE OF CAPITALISM

Author – John Dewey

HOW WE THINK & FREEDOM AND CULTURE

Author – David Ricardo

PRINCIPLES OF POLITICAL ECONOMY
AND TAXATION

Author – Thomas Jefferson

BIOGRAPHY OF THOMAS JEFFERSON & THE
LIFE AND MORALS OF JESUS OF NAZARETH

Author – Emma Goldman

ANARCHISM AND OTHER WRITINGS

Author – Rosa Luxemburg

REFORM OR REVOLUTION & THE MASS STRIKE

Author – Leon Trotsky

THE REVOLUTION BETRAYED